This Book Belong To:

_____

_____

_____

_____

📅 Date: _____ 🕐 Time: _____

📍 Location: _____

Weather Conditions

☀ ☁ 🌤 🌧 🌦 🌨 🚩 🌡
☐ ☐ ☐ ☐ ☐ ☐ _____ _____

Firearm:	
Bullet:	Seating Depth:
Powder:	Grains:
Primer:	
Brass:	
Distance:	

Overall Results

☐ Poor ☐ Fair ☐ Good ☐ Excellent

Notes

_____

_____

_____

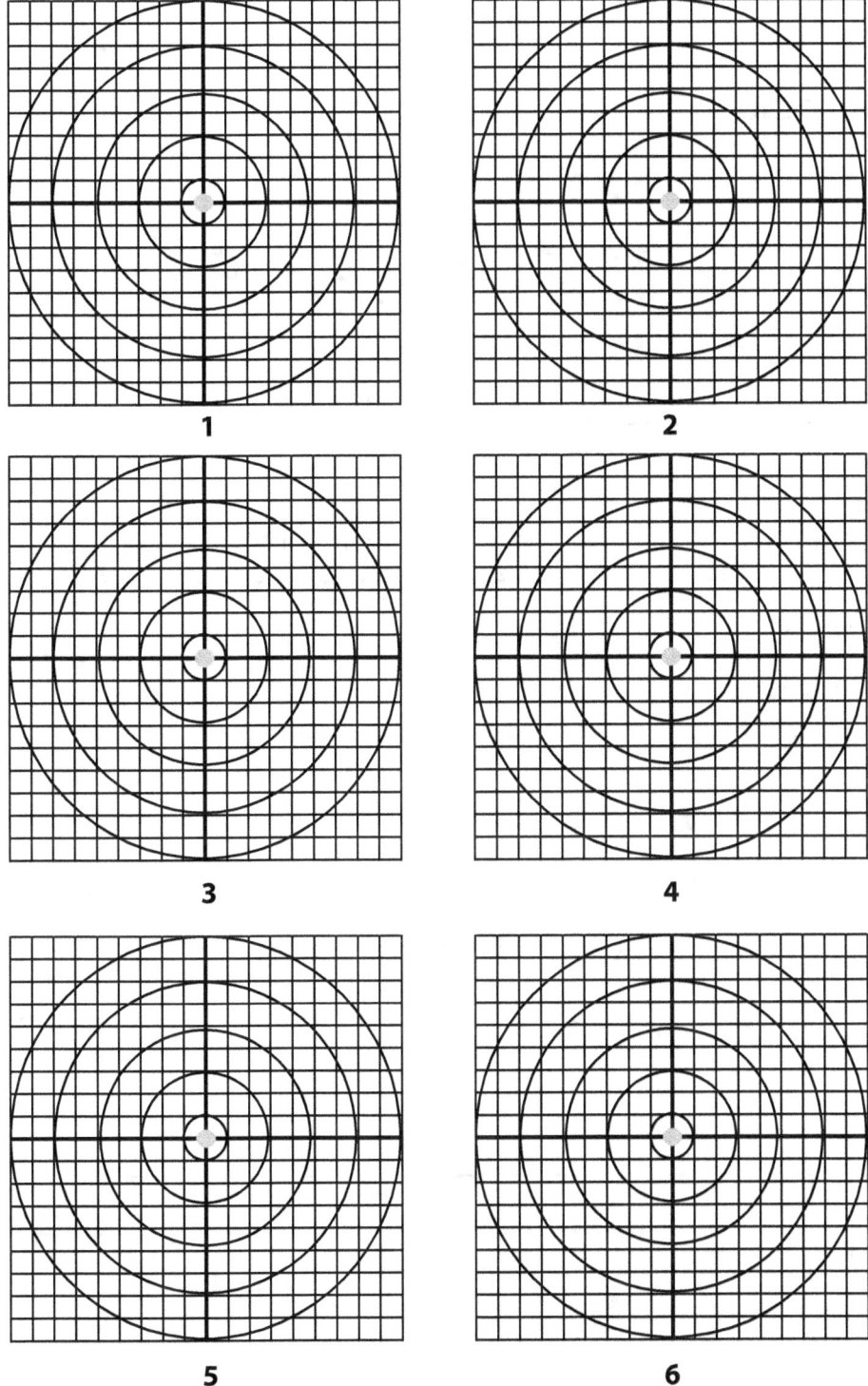

📅 Date: _____ 🕐 Time: _____

📍 Location: _____

Weather Conditions

☀️ ☁️ ⛅ 🌧️ 🌧️ 🌨️ 🚩 🌡️
☐   ☐   ☐   ☐   ☐   ☐   ___ ___

Firearm:	
Bullet:	Seating Depth:
Powder:	Grains:
Primer:	
Brass:	
Distance:	

Overall Results

☐ Poor   ☐ Fair   ☐ Good   ☐ Excellent

Notes

_____

_____

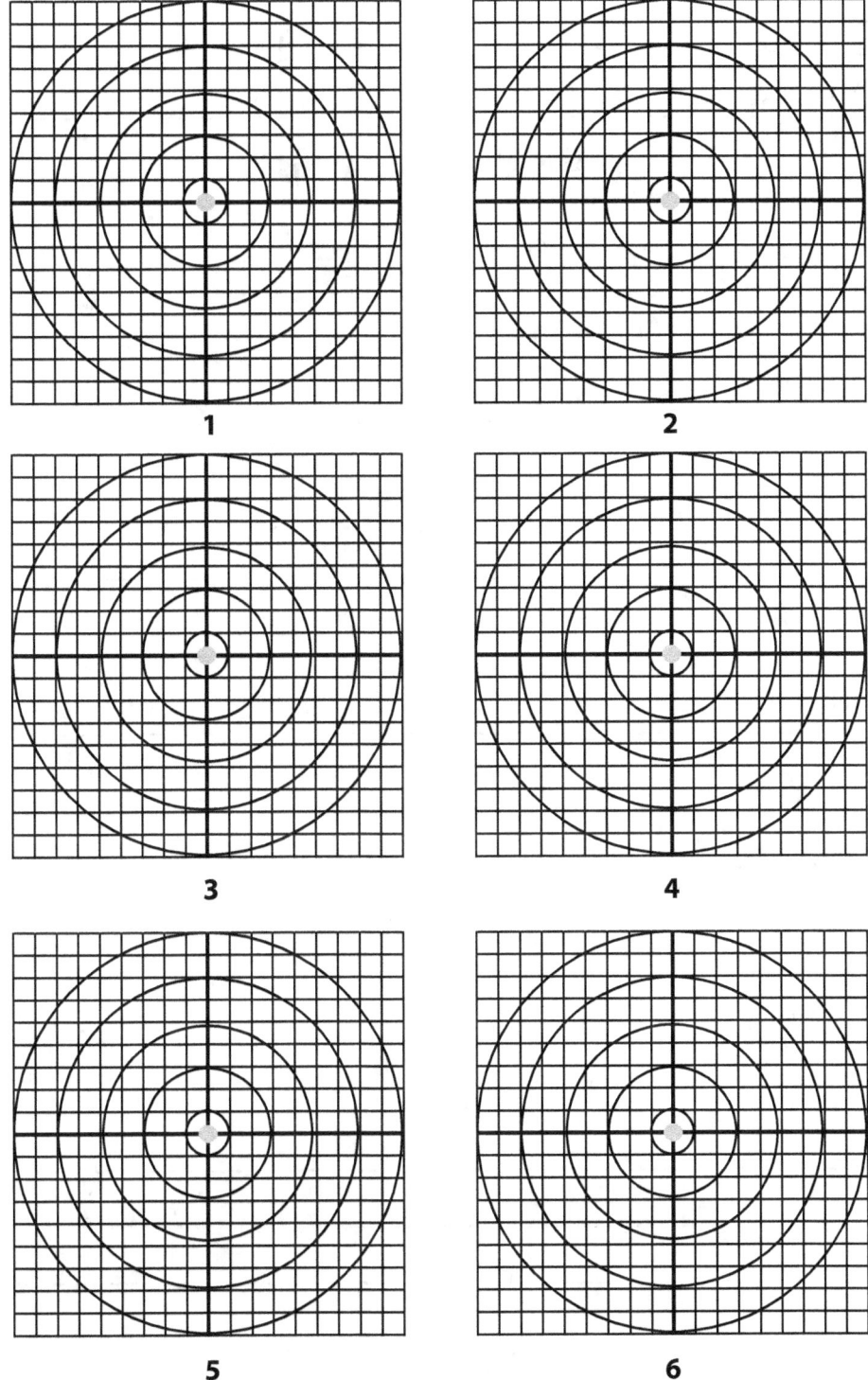

📅 Date: _____ 🕐 Time: _____

📍 Location: _____

Weather Conditions

☀ ☁ 🌤 🌧 🌧 🌨 ⚑ 🌡
☐ ☐ ☐ ☐ ☐ ☐ ____ ____

Firearm:	
Bullet:	Seating Depth:
Powder:	Grains:
Primer:	
Brass:	
Distance:	

Overall Results

☐ Poor   ☐ Fair   ☐ Good   ☐ Excellent

Notes

_____
_____

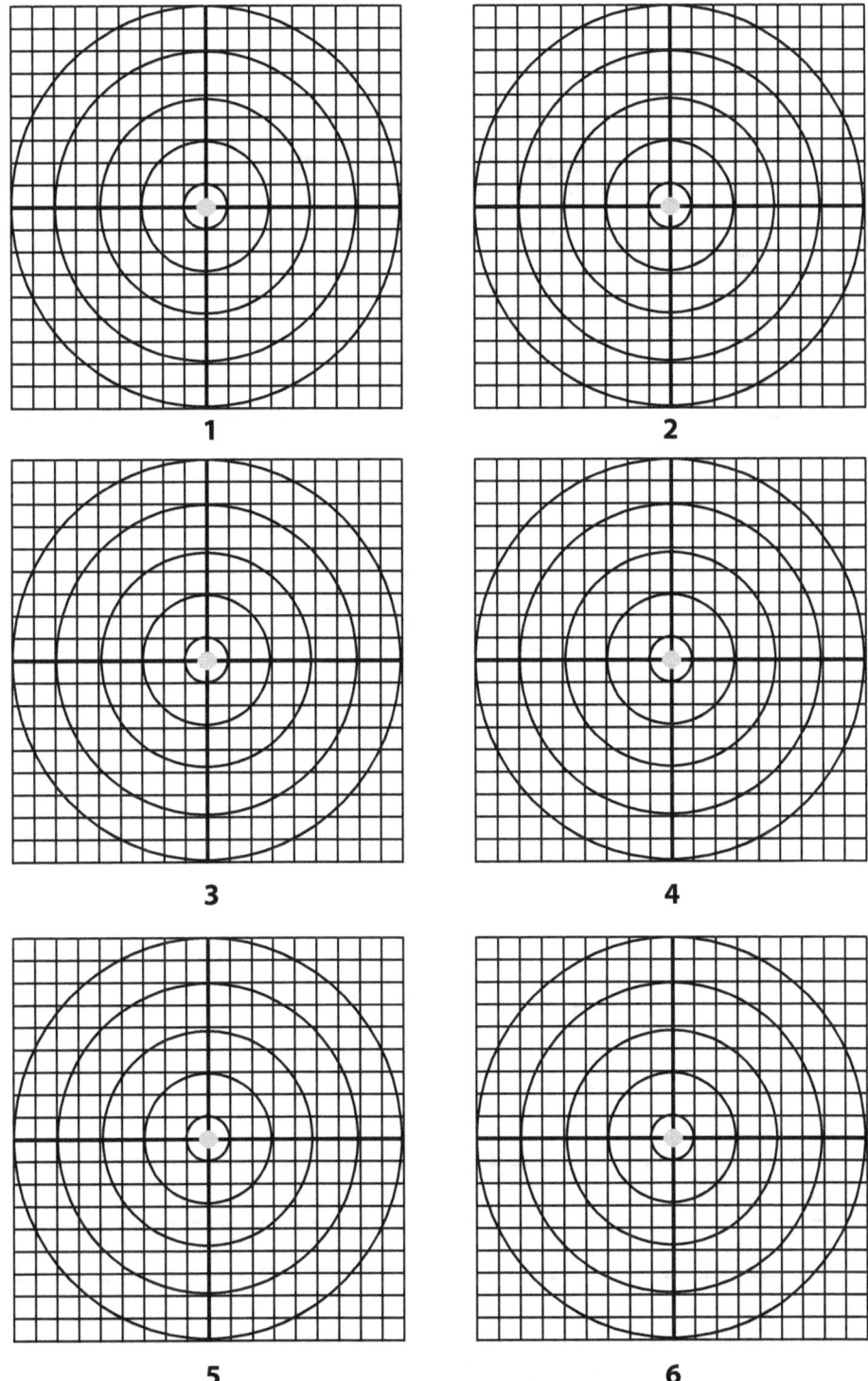

📅 Date: _____ 🕐 Time: _____

📍 Location: _____

Weather Conditions

☀ ☐   ⛅ ☐   🌥 ☐   🌧 ☐   🌧 ☐   🌨 ☐   🚩 _____   🌡 _____

Firearm:	
Bullet:	Seating Depth:
Powder:	Grains:
Primer:	
Brass:	
Distance:	

Overall Results

☐ Poor   ☐ Fair   ☐ Good   ☐ Excellent

Notes

_____

_____

_____

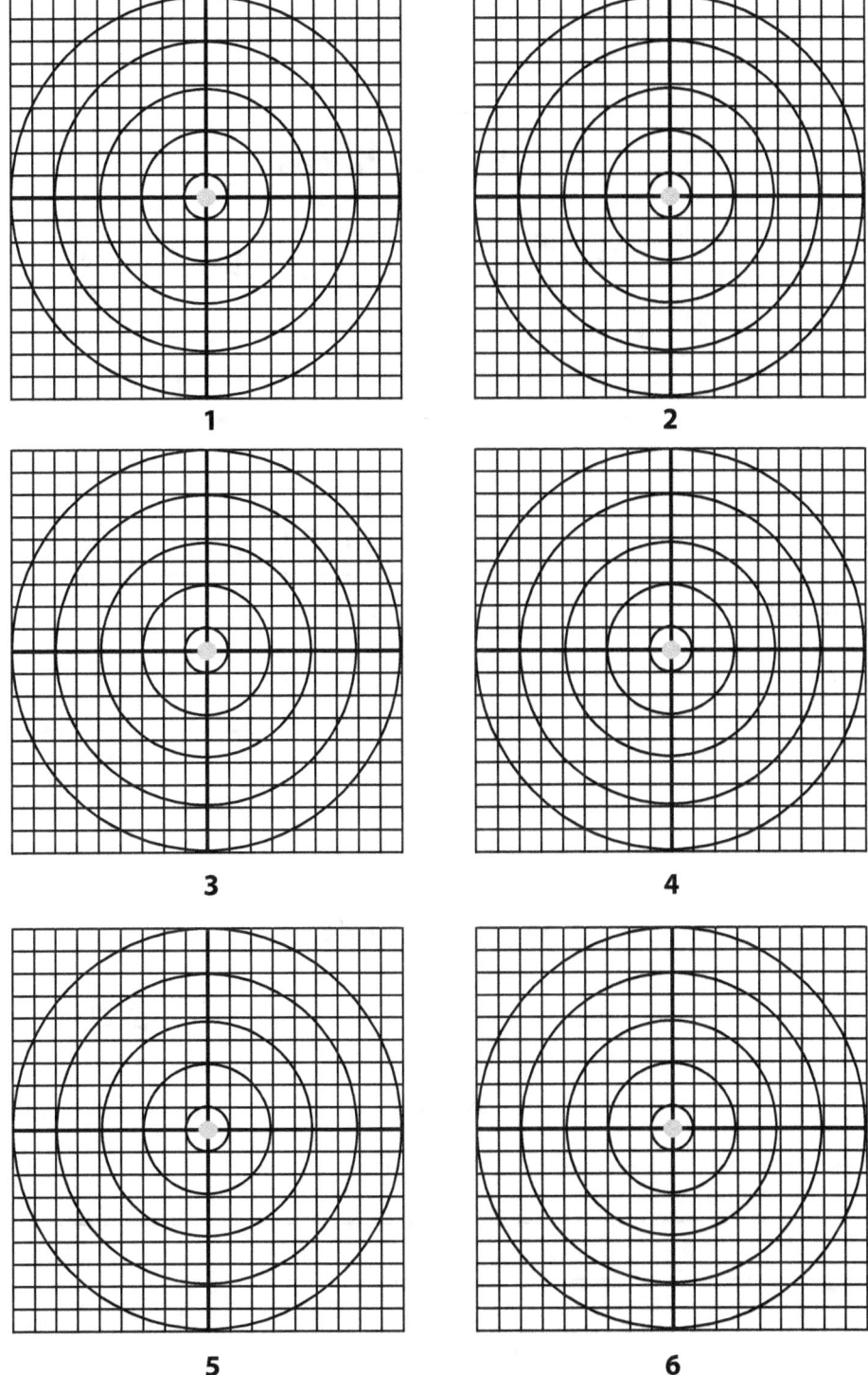

Date: _____ Time: _____

Location: _____

Weather Conditions

☀ ☁ ⛅ 🌧 🌧 🌨 ⚑ 🌡

☐ ☐ ☐ ☐ ☐ ☐ _____ _____

Firearm:	
Bullet:	Seating Depth:
Powder:	Grains:
Primer:	
Brass:	
Distance:	

Overall Results

☐ Poor   ☐ Fair   ☐ Good   ☐ Excellent

Notes

_____

_____

_____

☆ ☆ ☆ ☆ ☆

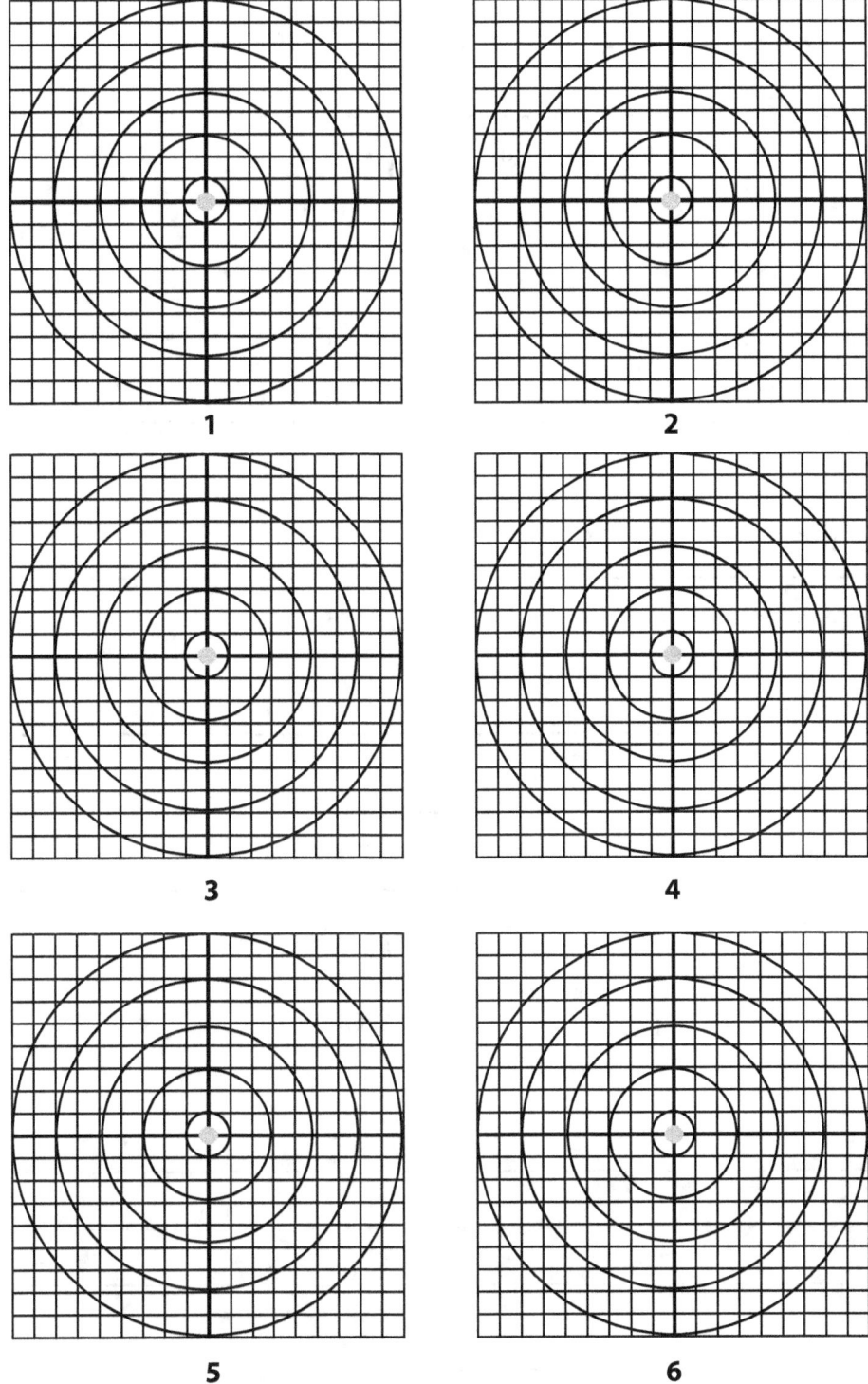

📅 Date: _____   🕐 Time: _____

📍 Location: _____

Weather Conditions

☀ ☁ 🌤 🌧 🌧 🌨 🚩 🌡
☐ ☐ ☐ ☐ ☐ ☐ ___ ___

Firearm:	
Bullet:	Seating Depth:
Powder:	Grains:
Primer:	
Brass:	
Distance:	

Overall Results

☐ Poor   ☐ Fair   ☐ Good   ☐ Excellent

Notes

_____

_____

_____

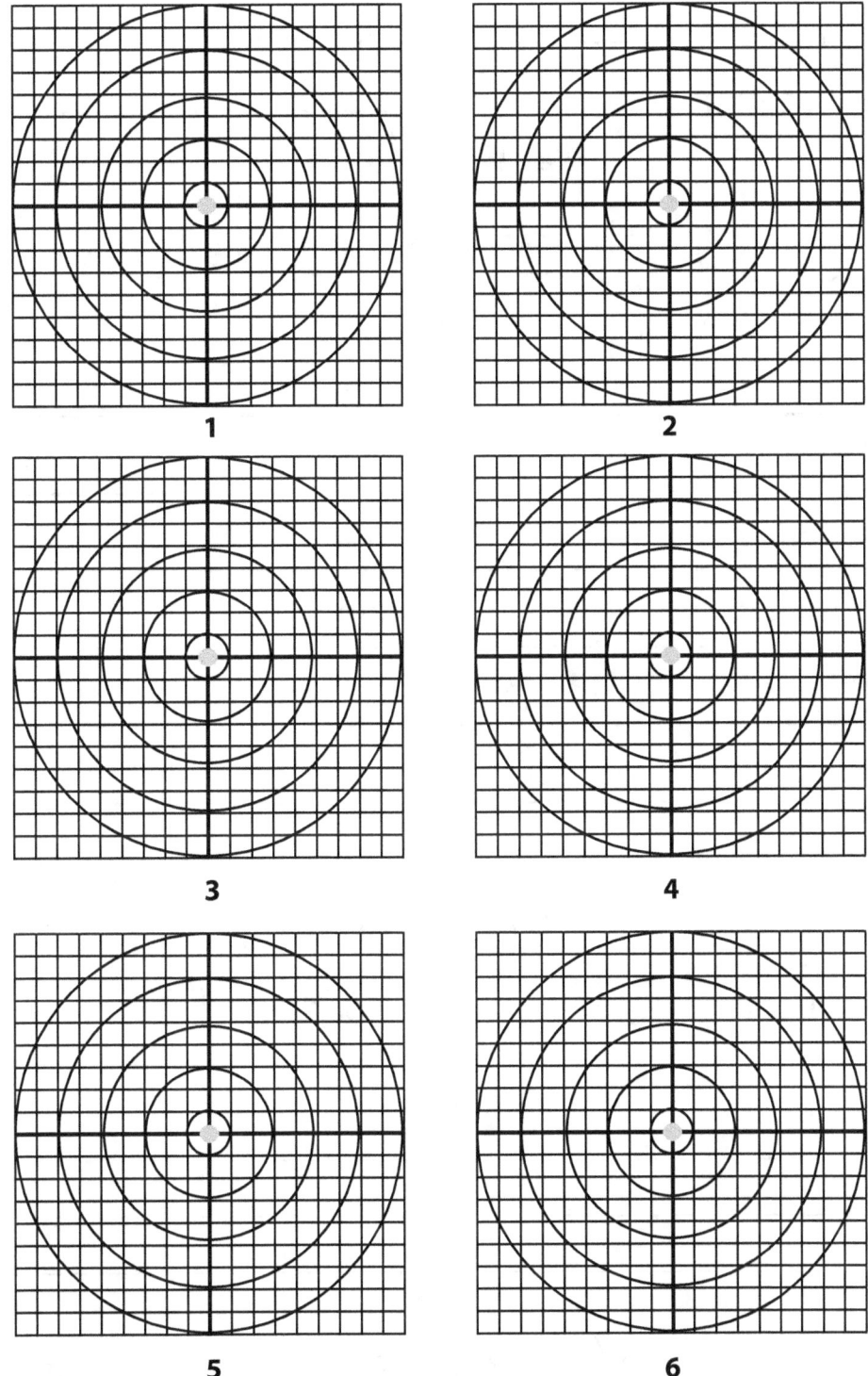

Date: _____   Time: _____

Location: _____

Weather Conditions

☀ ☐   ⛅ ☐   ☁ ☐   🌦 ☐   🌧 ☐   🌨 ☐   🚩 _____   🌡 _____

Firearm:	
Bullet:	Seating Depth:
Powder:	Grains:
Primer:	
Brass:	
Distance:	

Overall Results

☐ Poor   ☐ Fair   ☐ Good   ☐ Excellent

Notes

_____

_____

_____

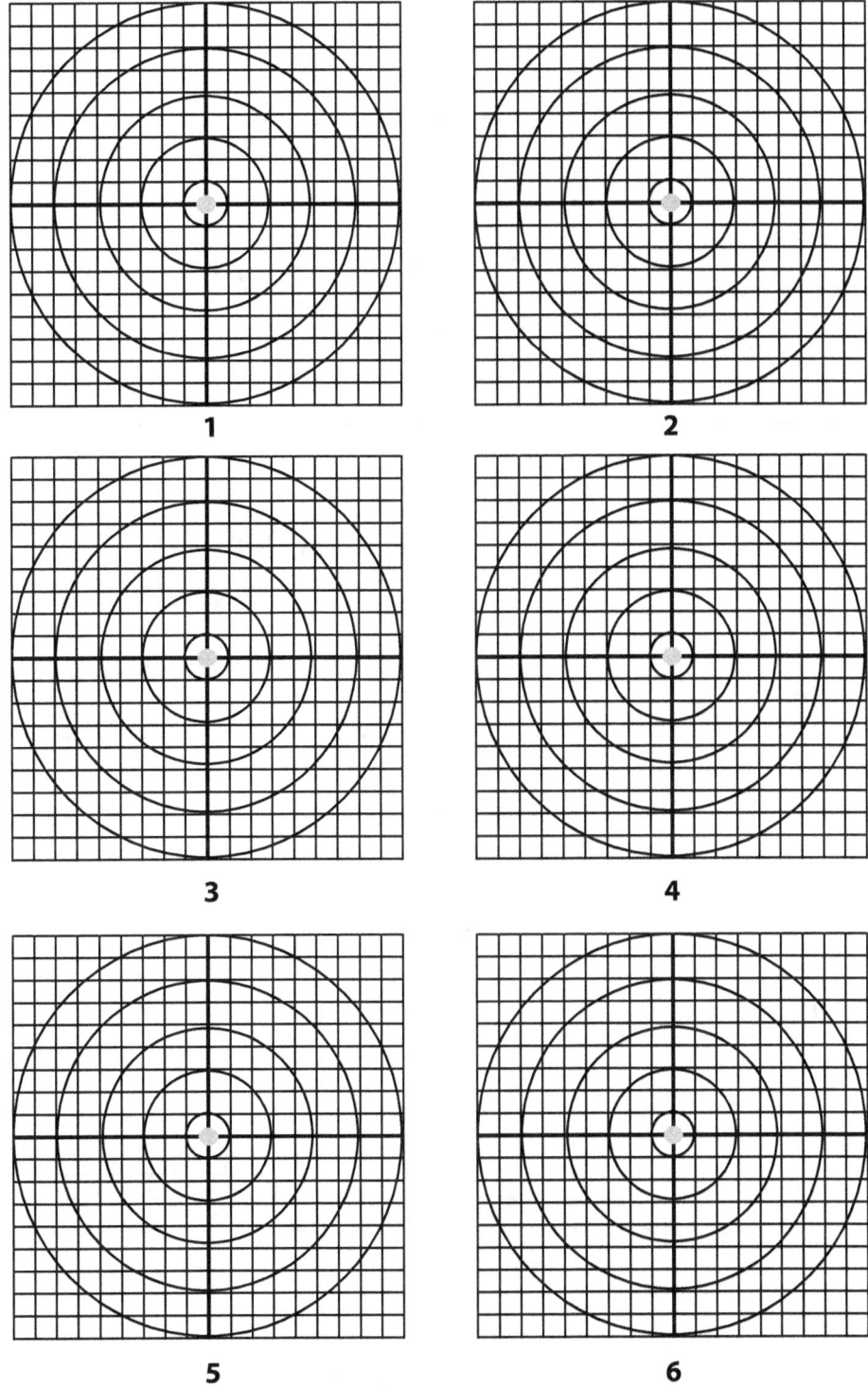

📅 Date: _____ 🕐 Time: _____

📍 Location: _____

Weather Conditions

☀ ☁ ⛅ 🌧 🌧 🌨 🚩 🌡
☐ ☐ ☐ ☐ ☐ ☐ ____ ____

Firearm:	
Bullet:	Seating Depth:
Powder:	Grains:
Primer:	
Brass:	
Distance:	

Overall Results

☐ Poor   ☐ Fair   ☐ Good   ☐ Excellent

Notes

_____

_____

_____

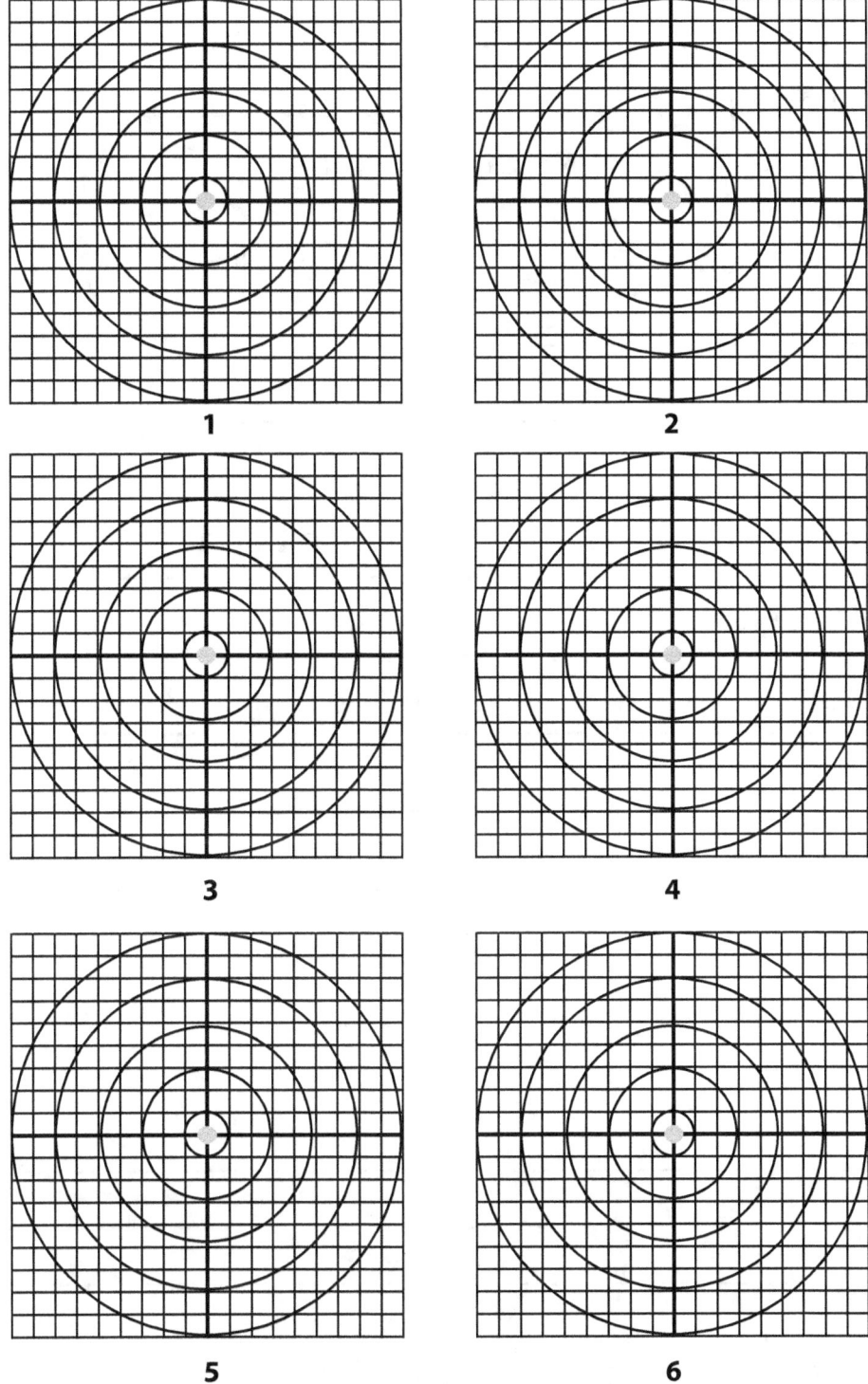

📅 Date: _____ 🕐 Time: _____

📍 Location: _____

Weather Conditions

☀️ ☁️ 🌤️ 🌧️ 🌧️ 🌨️ 🚩 🌡️
☐   ☐   ☐   ☐   ☐   ☐   _____

Firearm:	
Bullet:	Seating Depth:
Powder:	Grains:
Primer:	
Brass:	
Distance:	

Overall Results

☐ Poor   ☐ Fair   ☐ Good   ☐ Excellent

Notes

_____
_____
_____

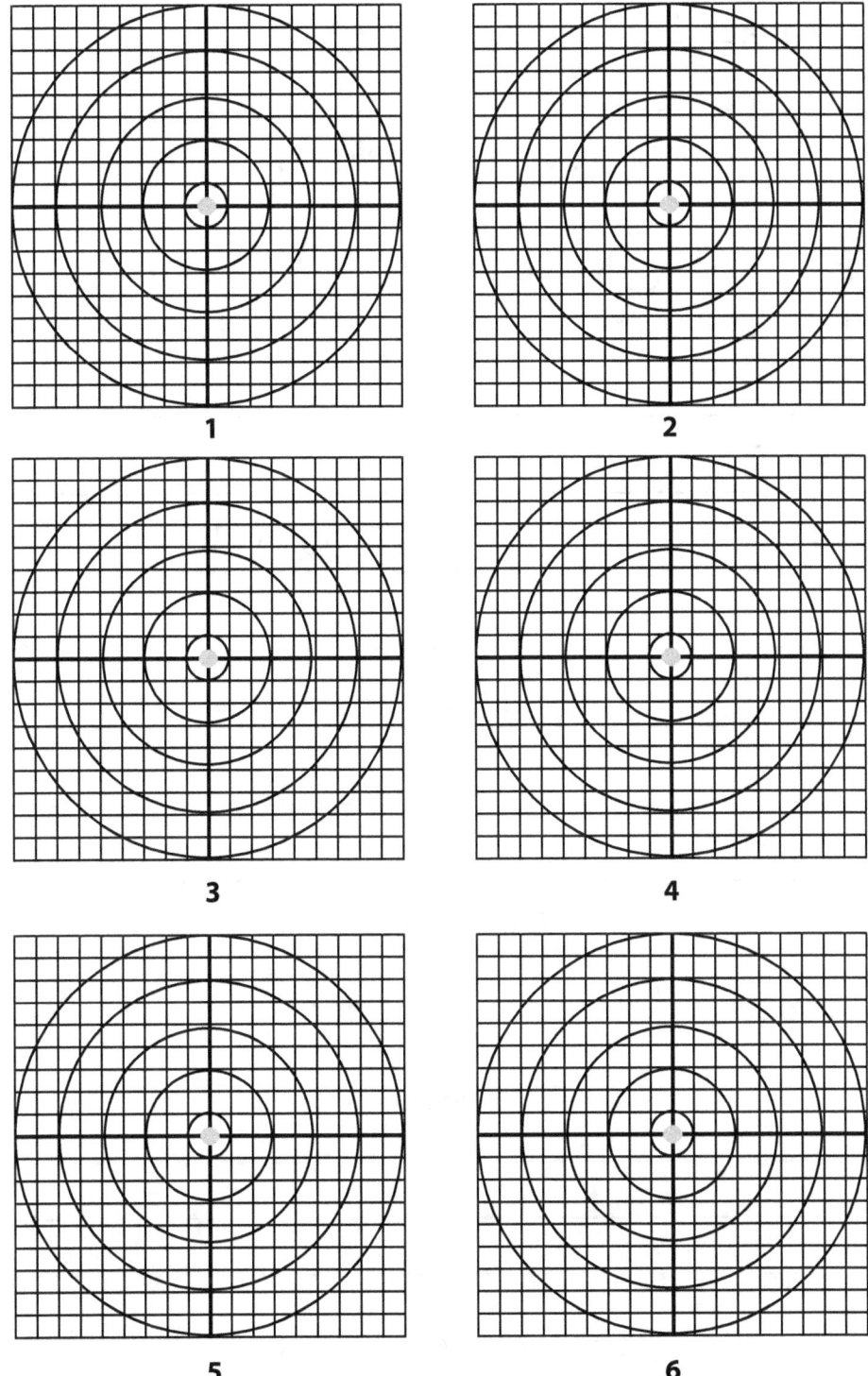

📅 Date: _____ 🕐 Time: _____

📍 Location: _____

Weather Conditions

☀ ☁ ⛅ 🌧 🌧 ❄ 🚩 🌡
☐ ☐ ☐ ☐ ☐ ☐ _____ _____

Firearm:	
Bullet:	Seating Depth:
Powder:	Grains:
Primer:	
Brass:	
Distance:	

Overall Results

☐ Poor   ☐ Fair   ☐ Good   ☐ Excellent

Notes

_____

_____

_____

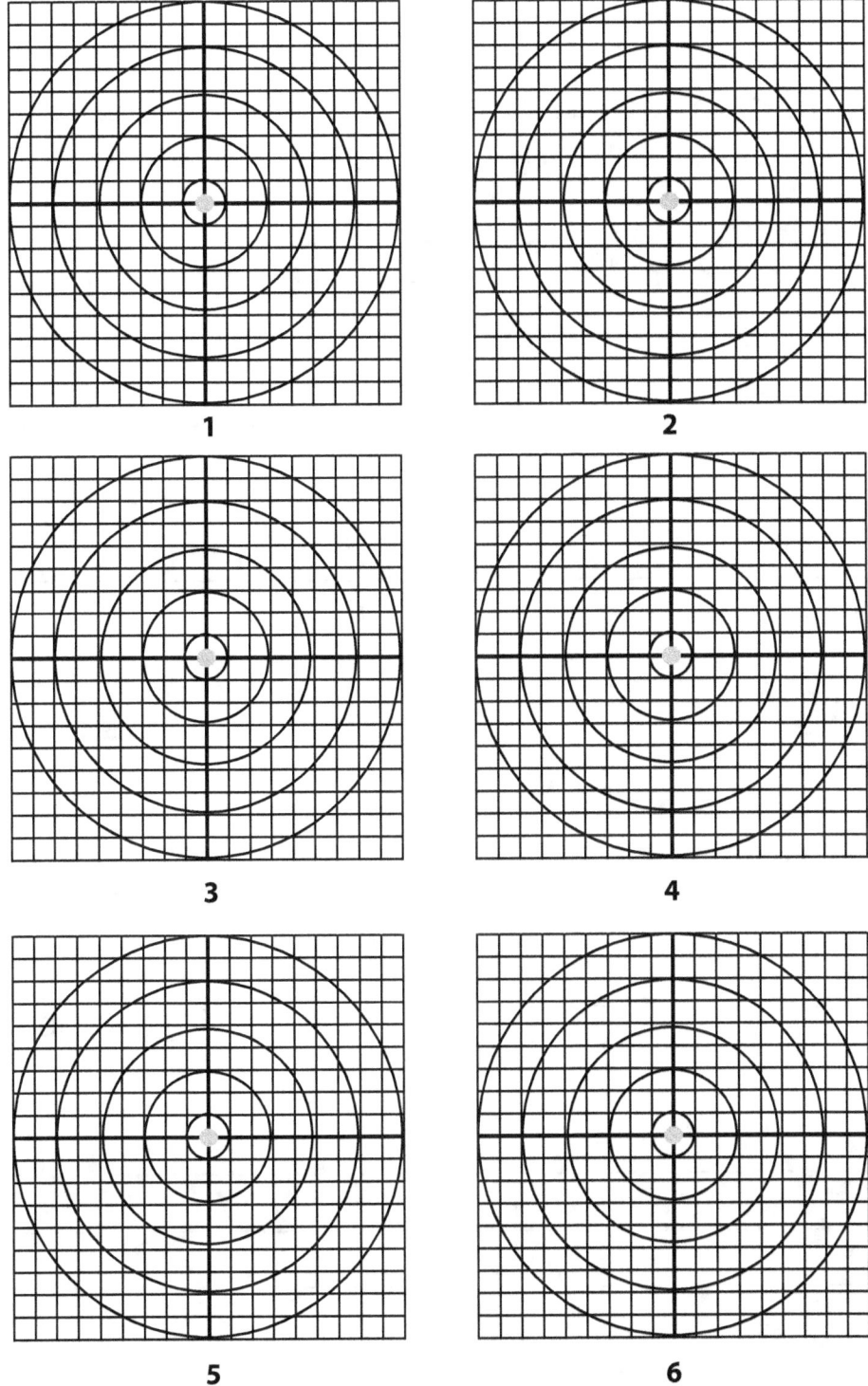

Date: _____   🕒 Time: _____
📍 Location: _____

Weather Conditions

☀️ ☁️ ⛅ 🌦️ 🌧️ 🌨️   🚩 _____   🌡️ _____
☐   ☐   ☐   ☐   ☐   ☐

Firearm:	
Bullet:	Seating Depth:
Powder:	Grains:
Primer:	
Brass:	
Distance:	

Overall Results

☐ Poor   ☐ Fair   ☐ Good   ☐ Excellent

Notes

_____
_____
_____

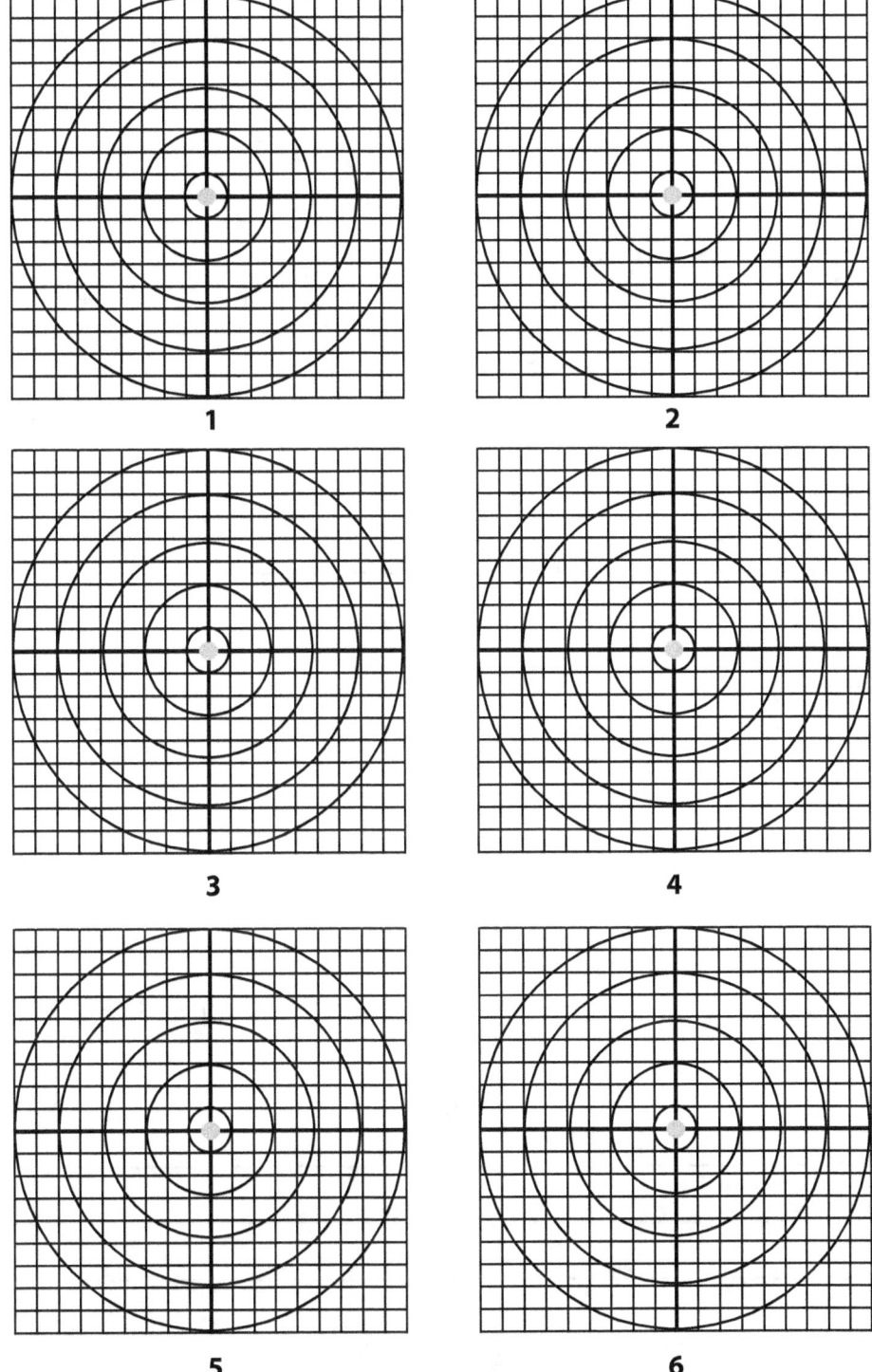

Date: _____ Time: _____

Location: _____

Weather Conditions

☀ ☁ 🌤 🌧 🌧 🌨 🚩 🌡

☐ ☐ ☐ ☐ ☐ ☐ _____ _____

Firearm:	
Bullet:	Seating Depth:
Powder:	Grains:
Primer:	
Brass:	
Distance:	

Overall Results

☐ Poor   ☐ Fair   ☐ Good   ☐ Excellent

Notes

_____

_____

_____

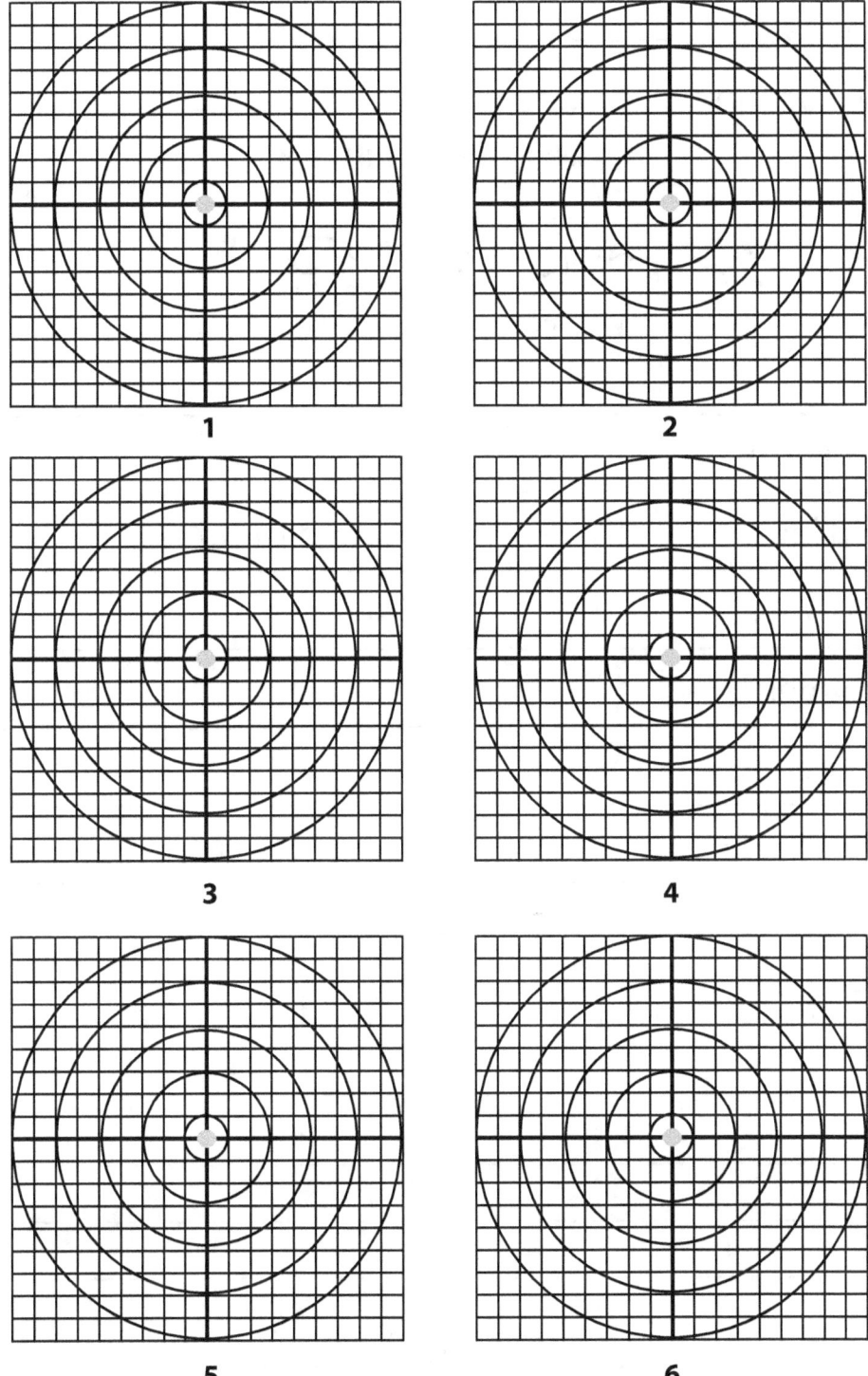

📅 Date: _____ 🕐 Time: _____

📍 Location: _____

Weather Conditions

☀️ ☁️ ⛅ 🌧️ 🌧️ 🌨️ 🚩_____ 🌡️_____
☐   ☐   ☐   ☐   ☐   ☐

Firearm:	
Bullet:	Seating Depth:
Powder:	Grains:
Primer:	
Brass:	
Distance:	

Overall Results

☐ Poor   ☐ Fair   ☐ Good   ☐ Excellent

Notes

_____

_____

_____

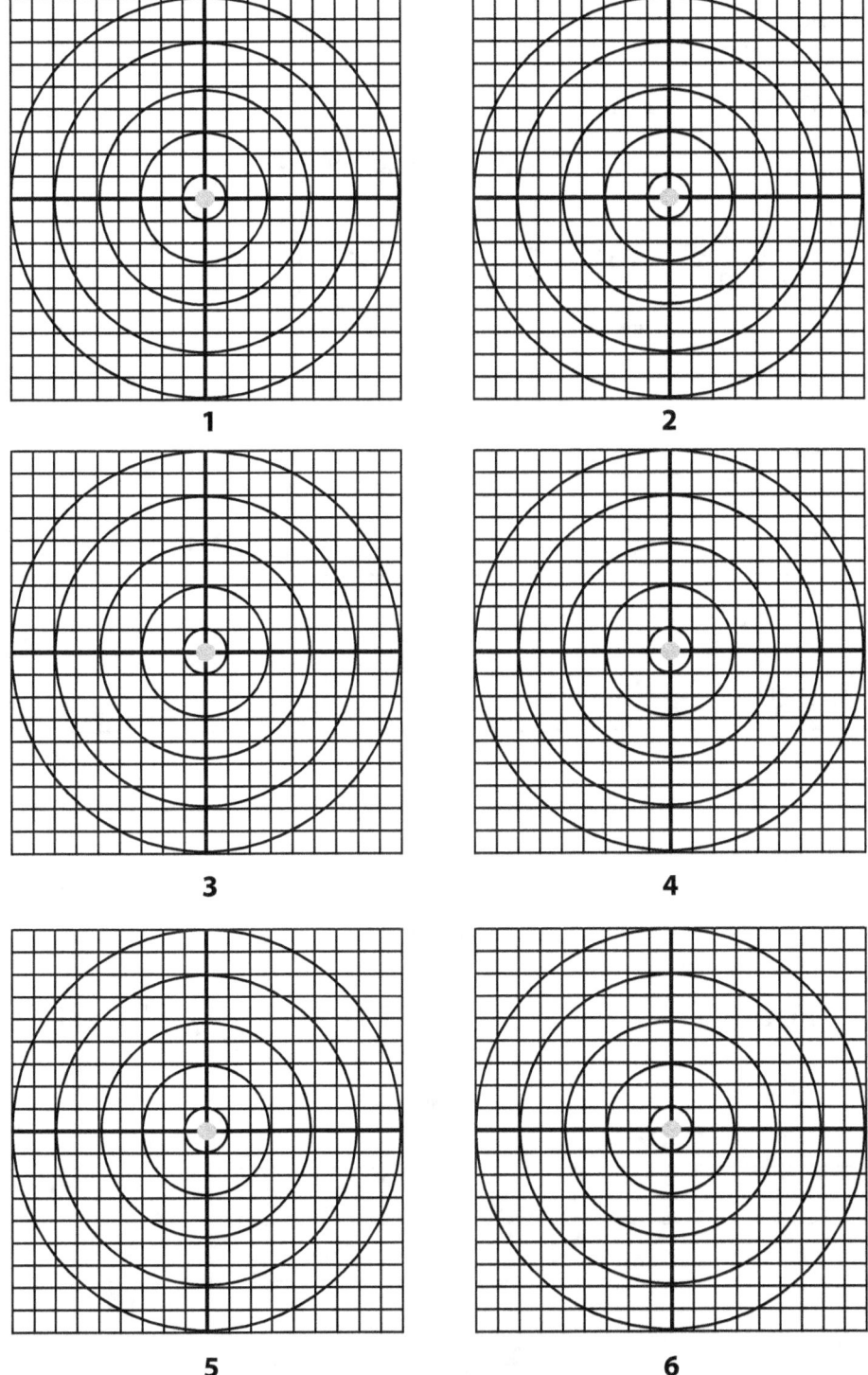

Date: _____ Time: _____

Location: _____

Weather Conditions

☀ ☁ ⛅ 🌧 🌧 🌨 🚩 🌡
☐ ☐ ☐ ☐ ☐ ☐

Firearm:	
Bullet:	Seating Depth:
Powder:	Grains:
Primer:	
Brass:	
Distance:	

Overall Results

☐ Poor ☐ Fair ☐ Good ☐ Excellent

Notes

_____
_____
_____

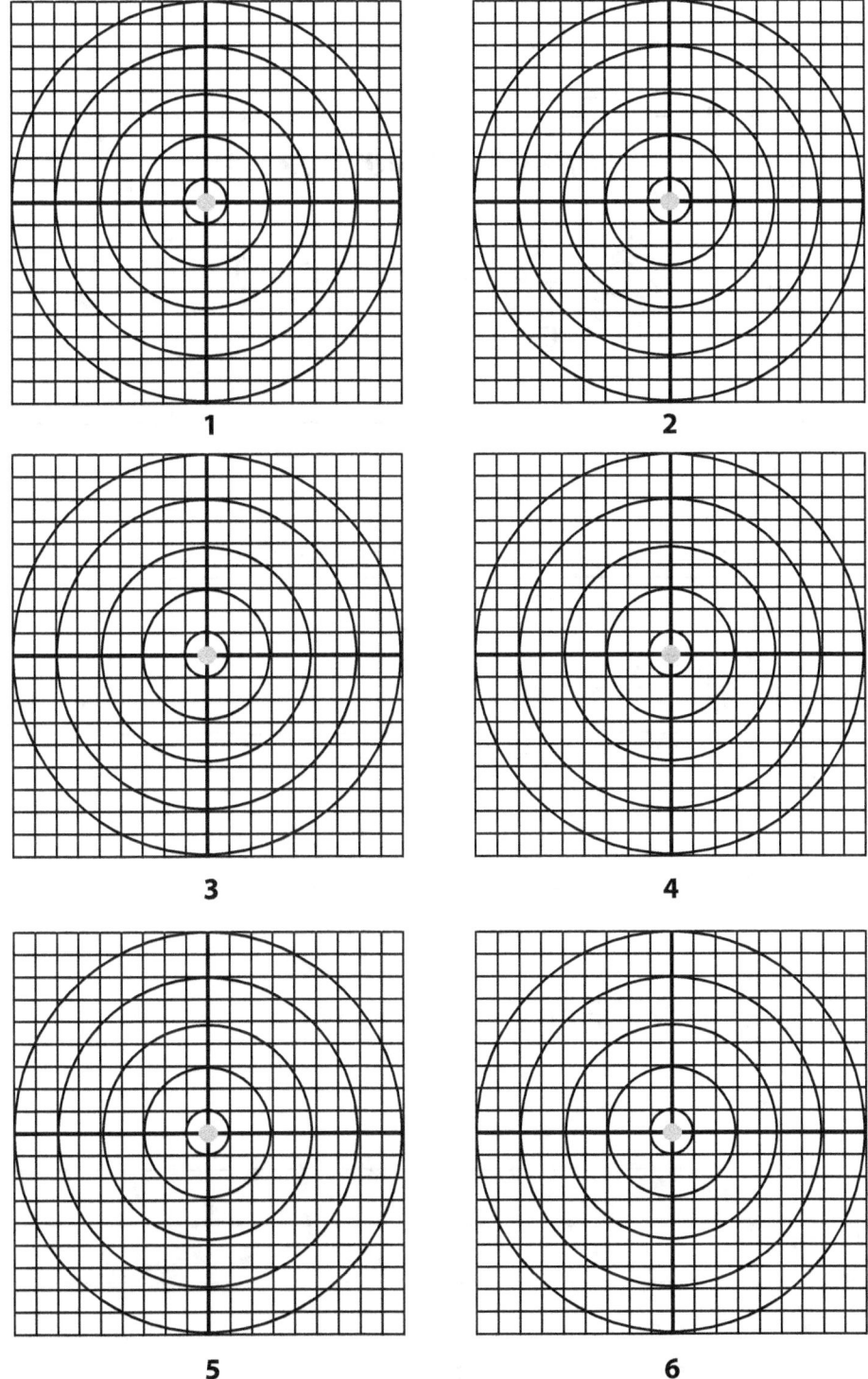

Date: _____ 🕐 Time: _____
Location: _____

Weather Conditions

☀ ☁ 🌤 🌧 🌧 🌨 🚩 🌡
☐ ☐ ☐ ☐ ☐ ☐ _____ _____

Firearm:	
Bullet:	Seating Depth:
Powder:	Grains:
Primer:	
Brass:	
Distance:	

Overall Results

☐ Poor ☐ Fair ☐ Good ☐ Excellent

Notes

_____
_____
_____

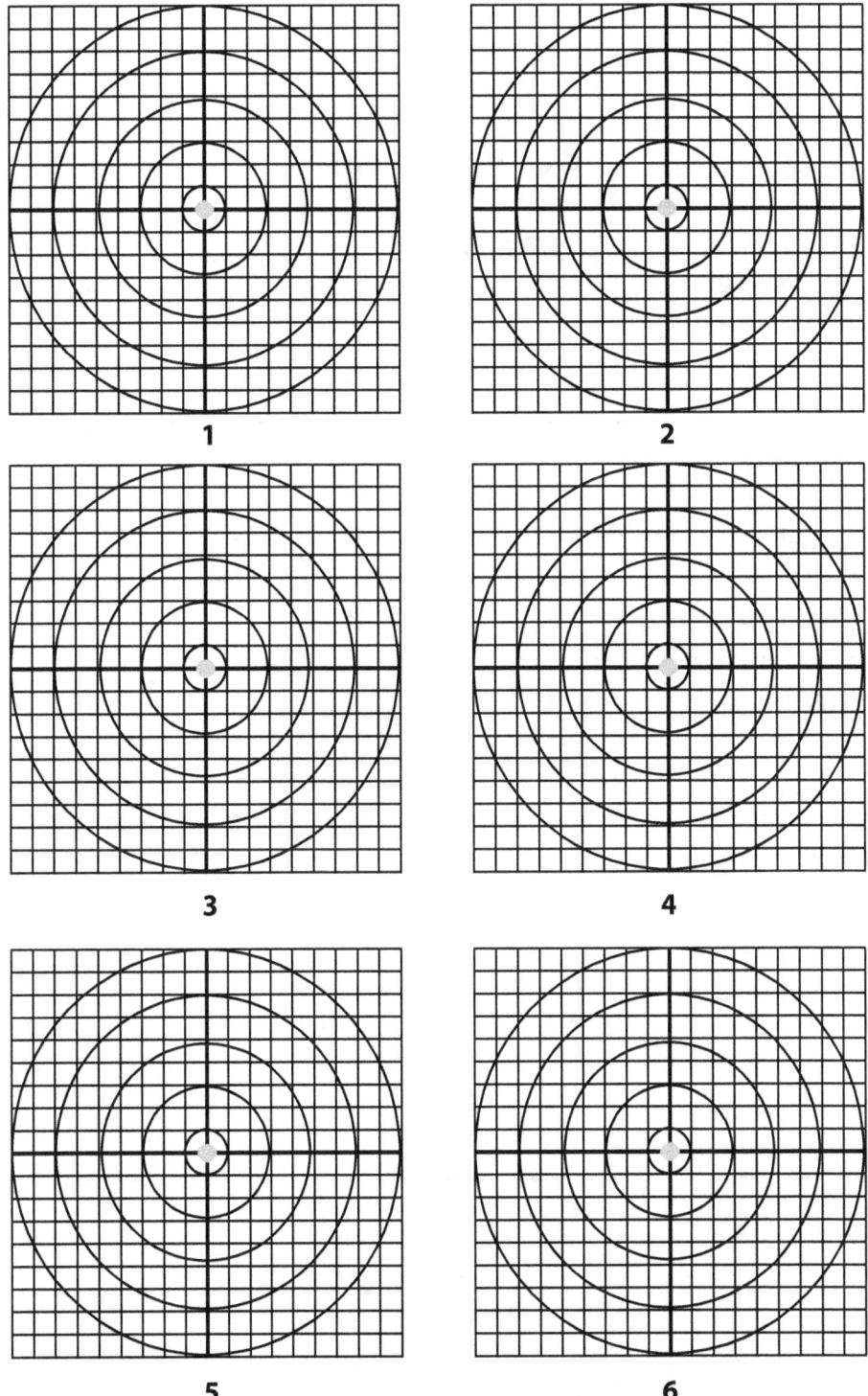

Date: _____ Time: _____

Location: _____

Weather Conditions

☐ ☐ ☐ ☐ ☐ ☐ _____ _____

Firearm:	
Bullet:	Seating Depth:
Powder:	Grains:
Primer:	
Brass:	
Distance:	

Overall Results

☐ Poor ☐ Fair ☐ Good ☐ Excellent

Notes

_____
_____
_____

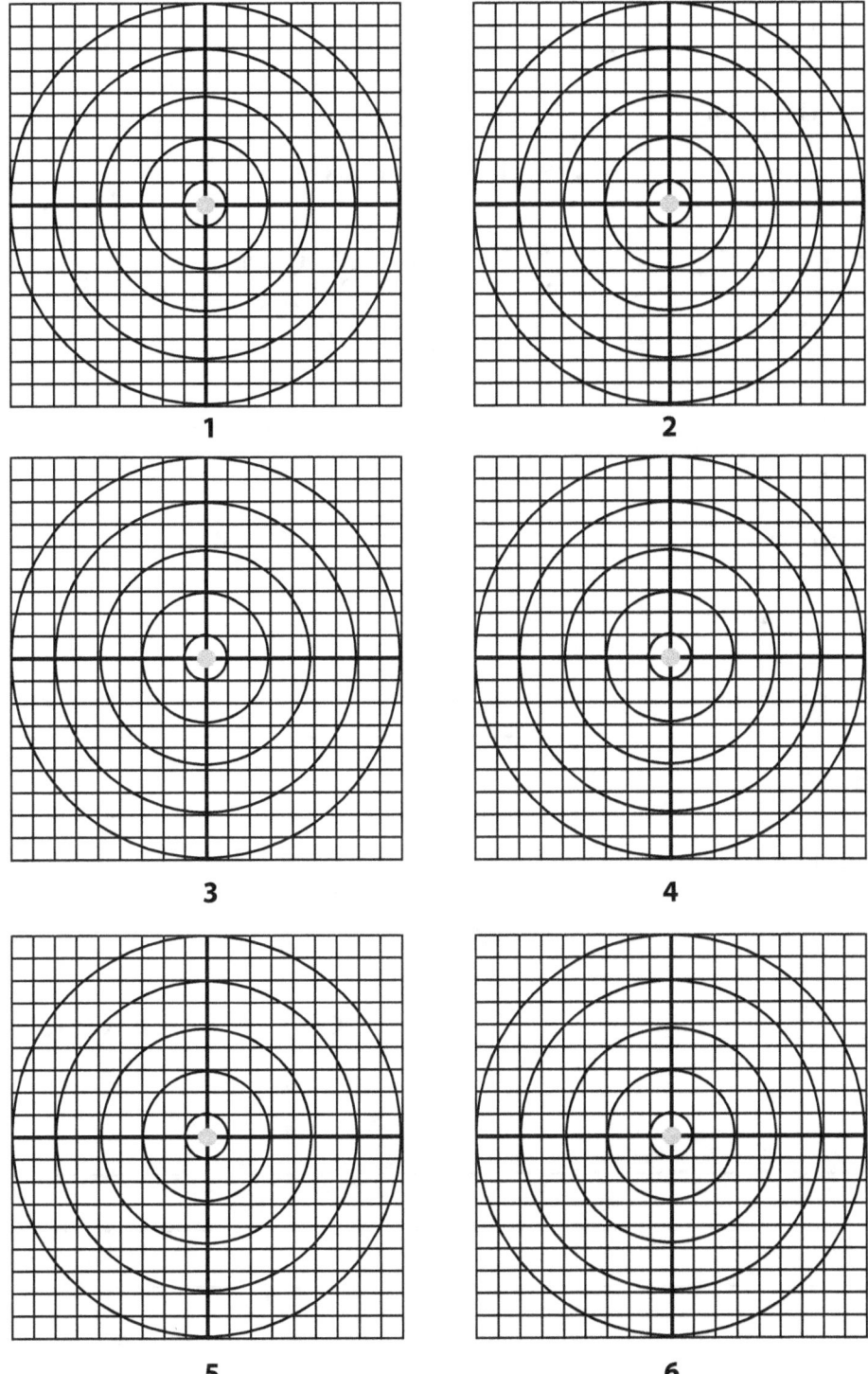

📅 Date: _____ 🕐 Time: _____

📍 Location: _____

Weather Conditions

☀️ ☁️ ⛅ 🌧️ 🌧️ 🌨️ 🚩 🌡️

☐ ☐ ☐ ☐ ☐ ☐ _____ _____

Firearm:	
Bullet:	Seating Depth:
Powder:	Grains:
Primer:	
Brass:	
Distance:	

Overall Results

☐ Poor   ☐ Fair   ☐ Good   ☐ Excellent

Notes

_____

_____

_____

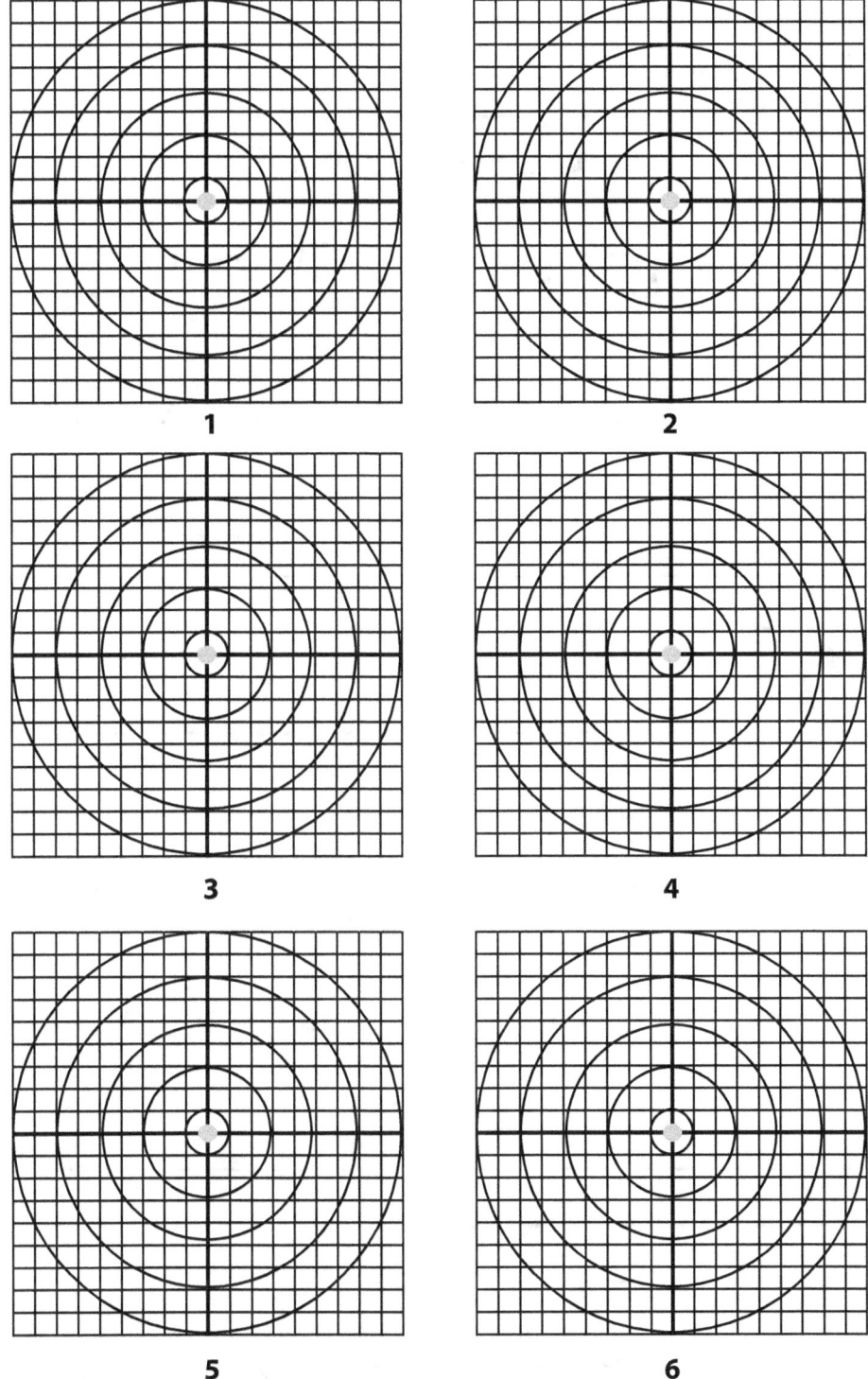

📅 Date: _____ 🕐 Time: _____

📍 Location: _____

Weather Conditions

☀ ☁ 🌤 🌧 🌨 🌨 🚩 🌡
☐   ☐   ☐   ☐   ☐   ☐   _____   _____

Firearm:	
Bullet:	Seating Depth:
Powder:	Grains:
Primer:	
Brass:	
Distance:	

Overall Results

☐ Poor   ☐ Fair   ☐ Good   ☐ Excellent

Notes

_____
_____
_____

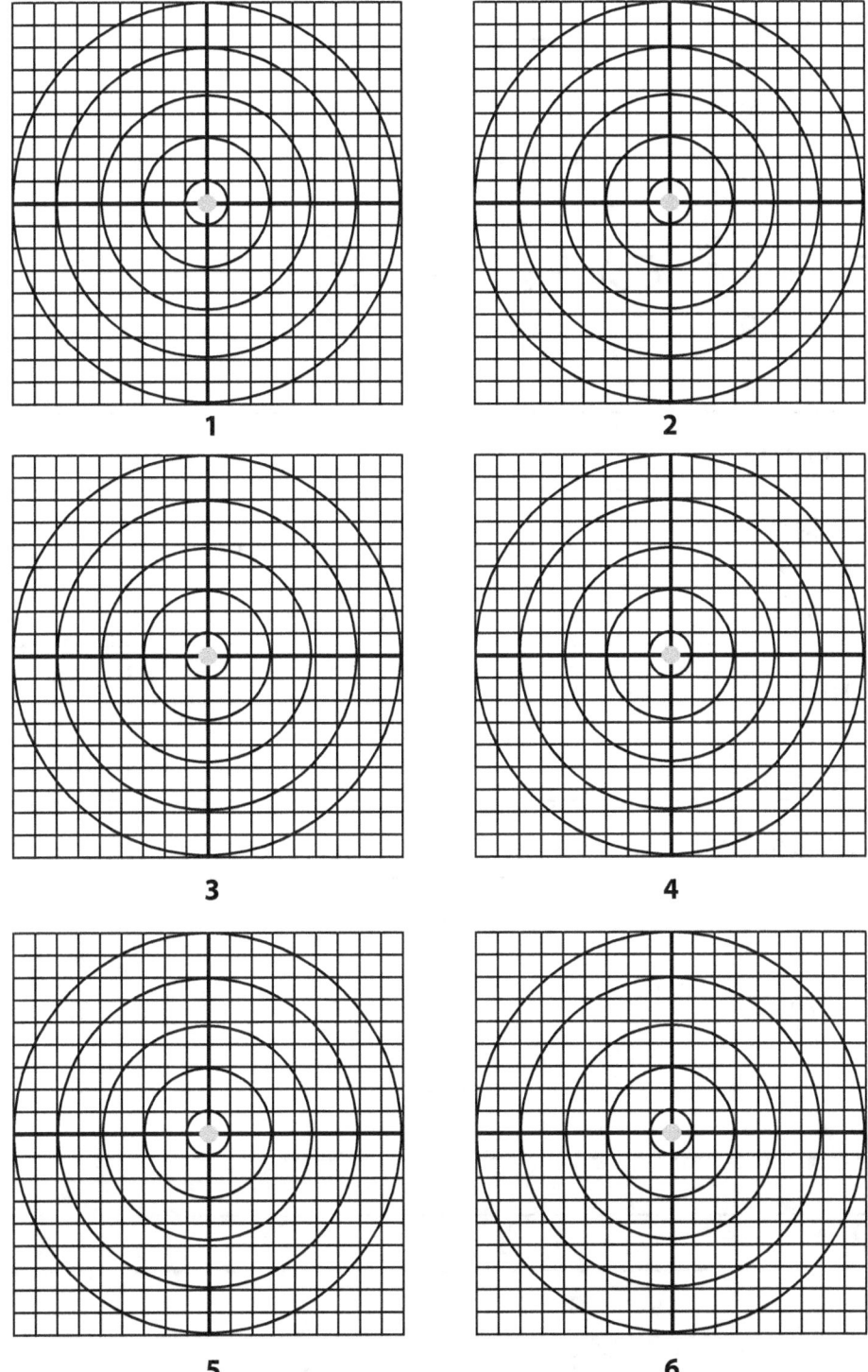

📅 Date: _____ 🕐 Time: _____

📍 Location: _____

Weather Conditions

☀ ☐   ⛅ ☐   ☁ ☐   🌧 ☐   🌧 ☐   🌨 ☐   🚩 _____   🌡 _____

Firearm:	
Bullet:	Seating Depth:
Powder:	Grains:
Primer:	
Brass:	
Distance:	

Overall Results

☐ Poor   ☐ Fair   ☐ Good   ☐ Excellent

Notes

_____

_____

_____

☆ ☆ ☆ ☆ ☆

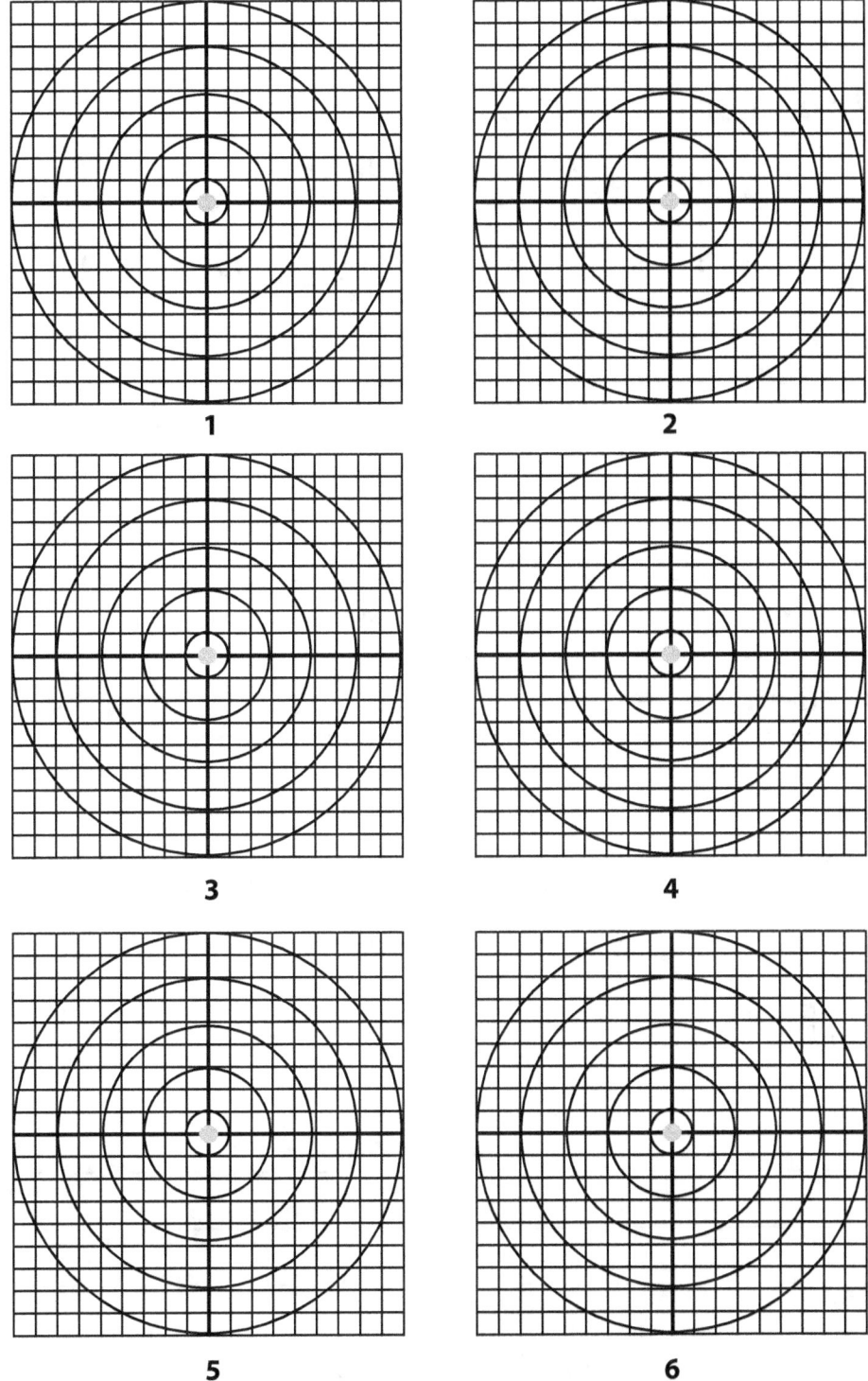

Date: _____ Time: _____

Location: _____

Weather Conditions

☀ ☁ ⛅ 🌧 🌧 🌨 🚩 🌡
☐ ☐ ☐ ☐ ☐ ☐ _____ _____

Firearm:	
Bullet:	Seating Depth:
Powder:	Grains:
Primer:	
Brass:	
Distance:	

Overall Results

☐ Poor   ☐ Fair   ☐ Good   ☐ Excellent

Notes

_____

_____

_____

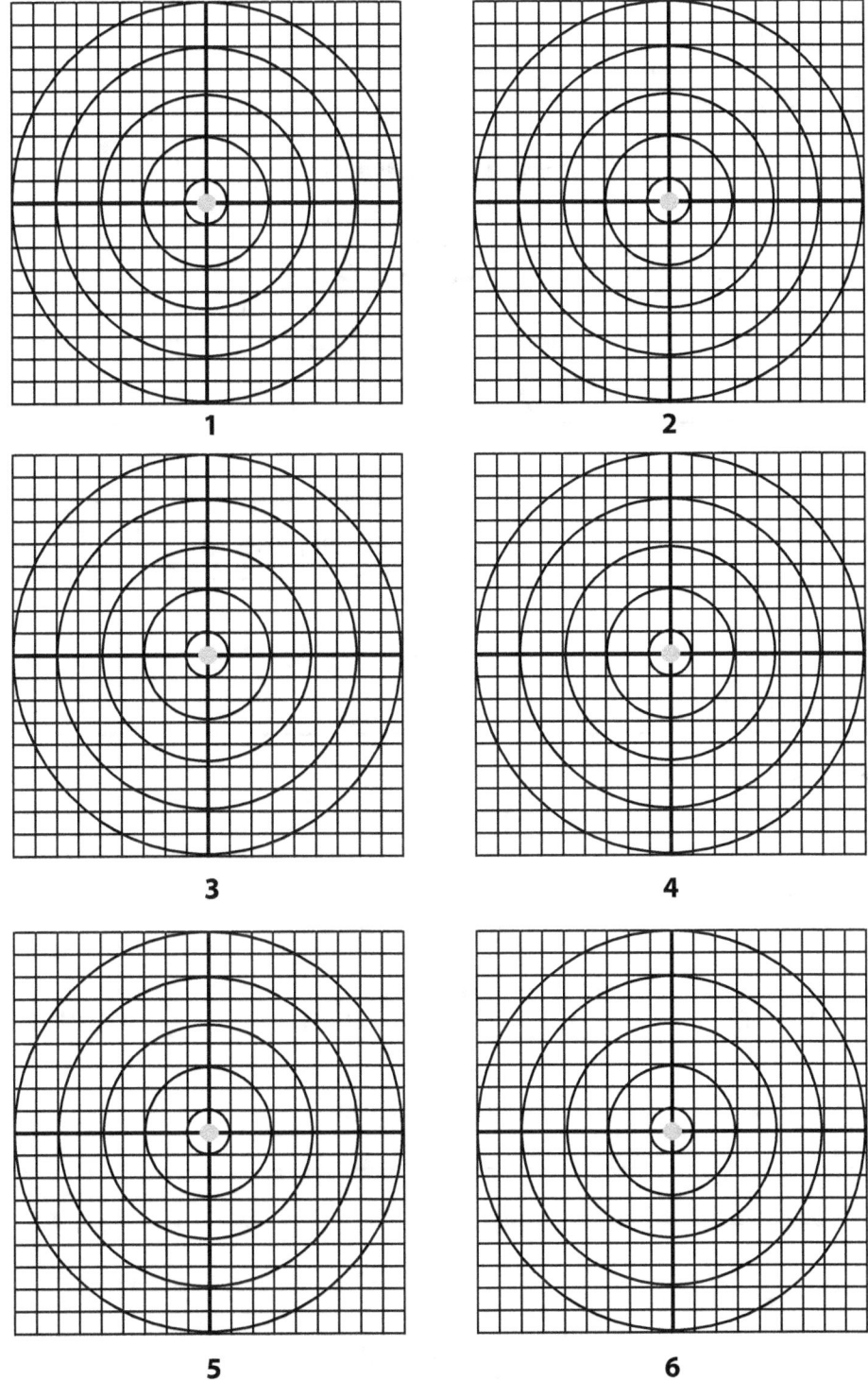

📅 Date: _____ 🕐 Time: _____

📍 Location: _____

Weather Conditions

☀ ☁ 🌤 🌧 🌧 🌨 ⛳ 🌡
☐   ☐   ☐   ☐   ☐   ☐   _____ _____

Firearm:	
Bullet:	Seating Depth:
Powder:	Grains:
Primer:	
Brass:	
Distance:	

Overall Results

☐ Poor   ☐ Fair   ☐ Good   ☐ Excellent

Notes

_____

_____

_____

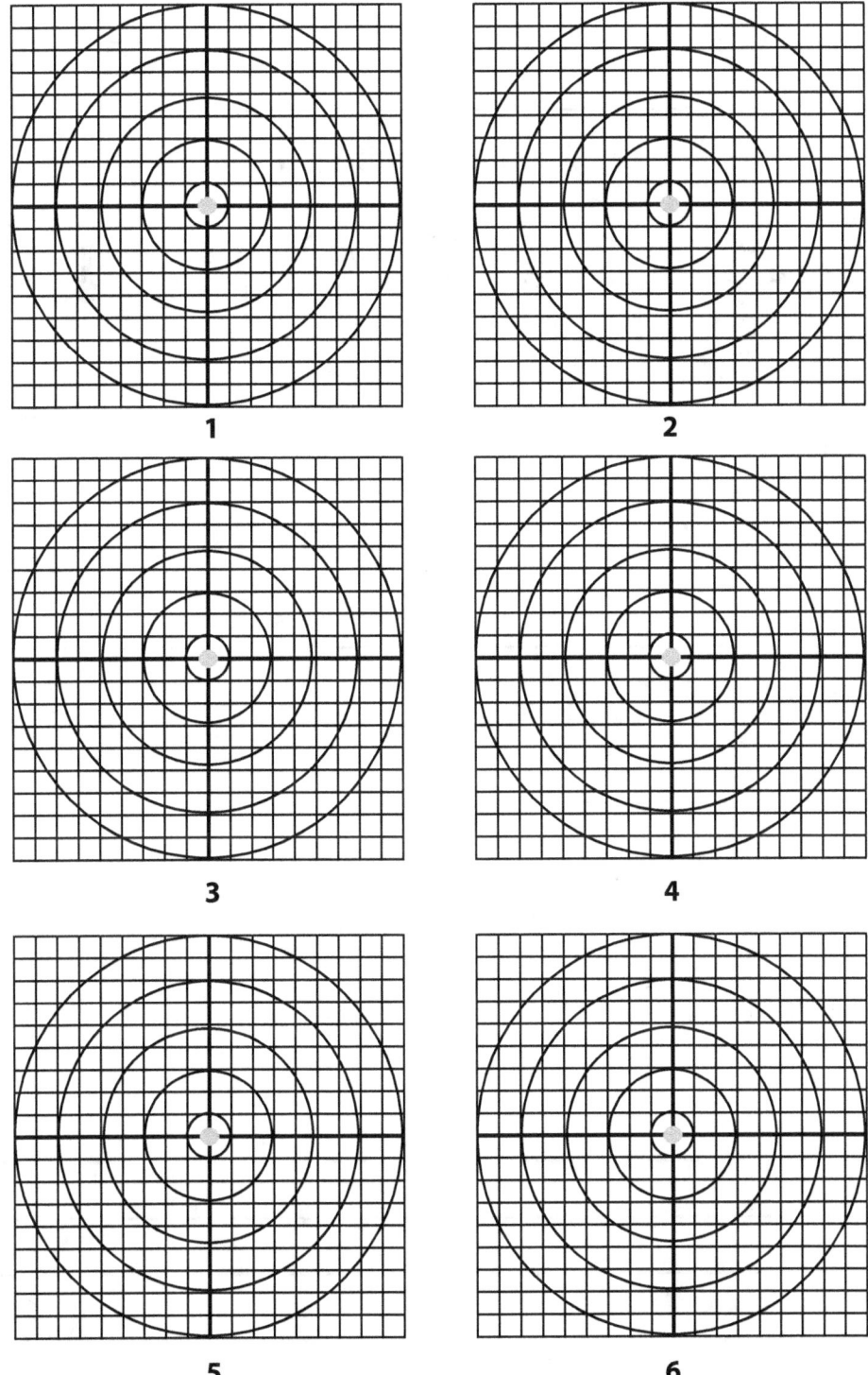

Date: _____ Time: _____

Location: _____

Weather Conditions

☐ ☀️ ☐ ⛅ ☐ ☁️ ☐ 🌧 ☐ 🌧 ☐ 🌨 ☐ 🚩 _____ ☐ 🌡 _____

Firearm:	
Bullet:	Seating Depth:
Powder:	Grains:
Primer:	
Brass:	
Distance:	

Overall Results

☐ Poor   ☐ Fair   ☐ Good   ☐ Excellent

Notes

_____

_____

_____

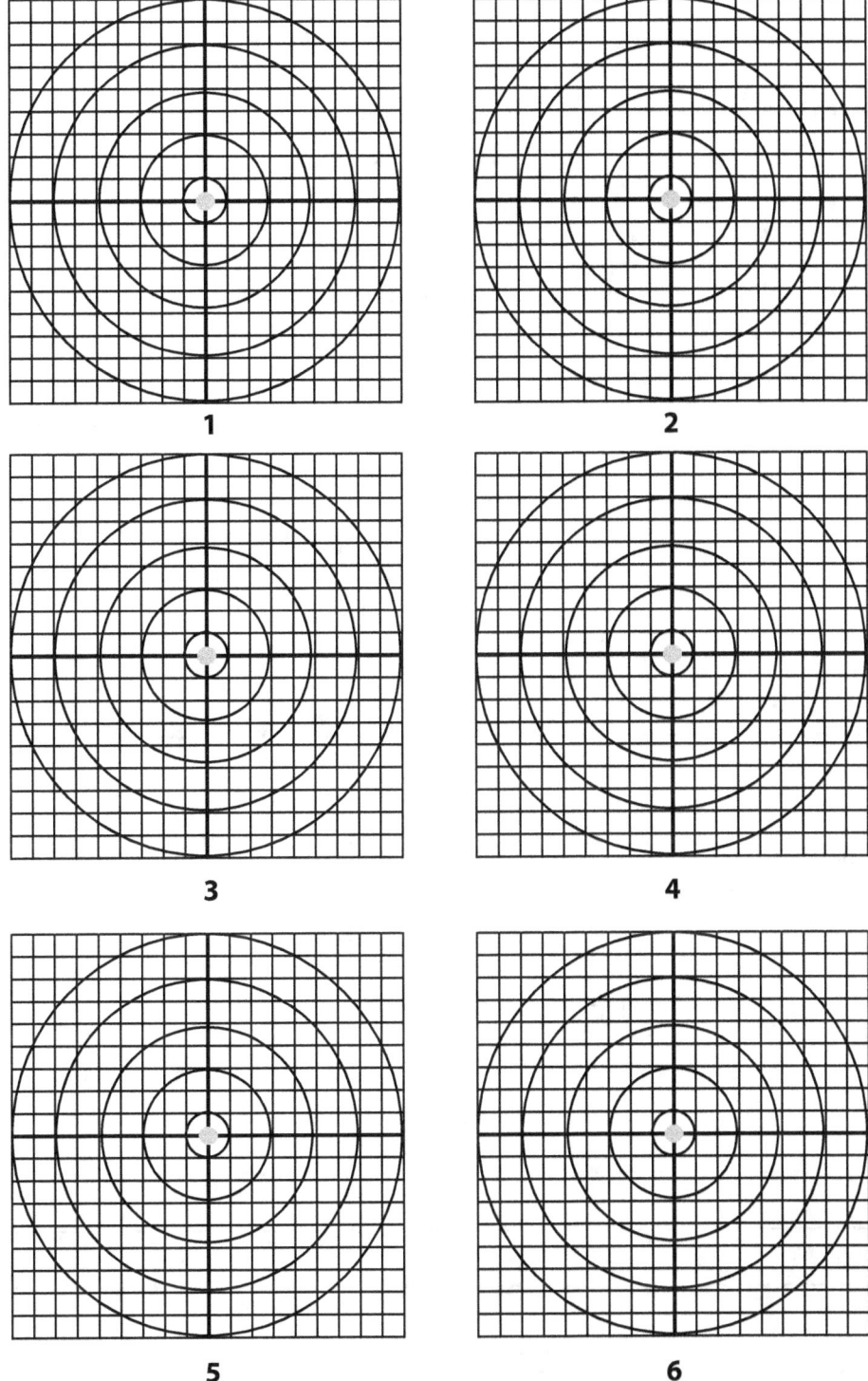

Date: _____ Time: _____
Location: _____

Weather Conditions

☀ ☁ ⛅ 🌧 🌧 🌨 🚩 🌡
☐   ☐   ☐   ☐   ☐   ☐   ___   ___

Firearm:	
Bullet:	Seating Depth:
Powder:	Grains:
Primer:	
Brass:	
Distance:	

Overall Results

☐ Poor   ☐ Fair   ☐ Good   ☐ Excellent

Notes

_____
_____
_____

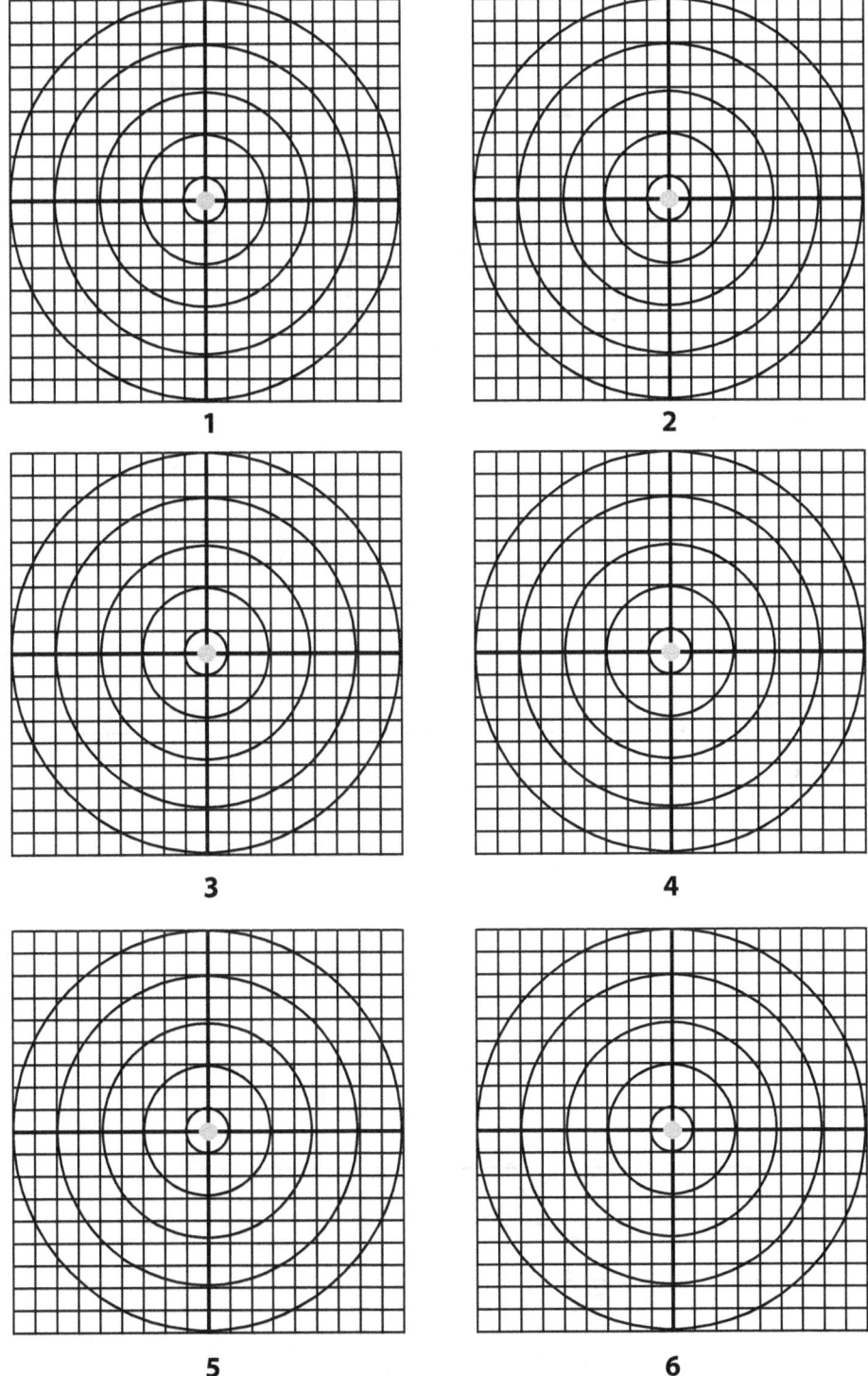

Date: _____ ⏰ Time: _____

 Location: _____

Weather Conditions

☀️ ☁️ 🌤️ 🌧️ 🌧️ 🌨️ 🚩 🌡️
☐ ☐ ☐ ☐ ☐ ☐ ___ ___

Firearm:	
Bullet:	Seating Depth:
Powder:	Grains:
Primer:	
Brass:	
Distance:	

Overall Results

☐ Poor ☐ Fair ☐ Good ☐ Excellent

Notes

_____
_____
_____

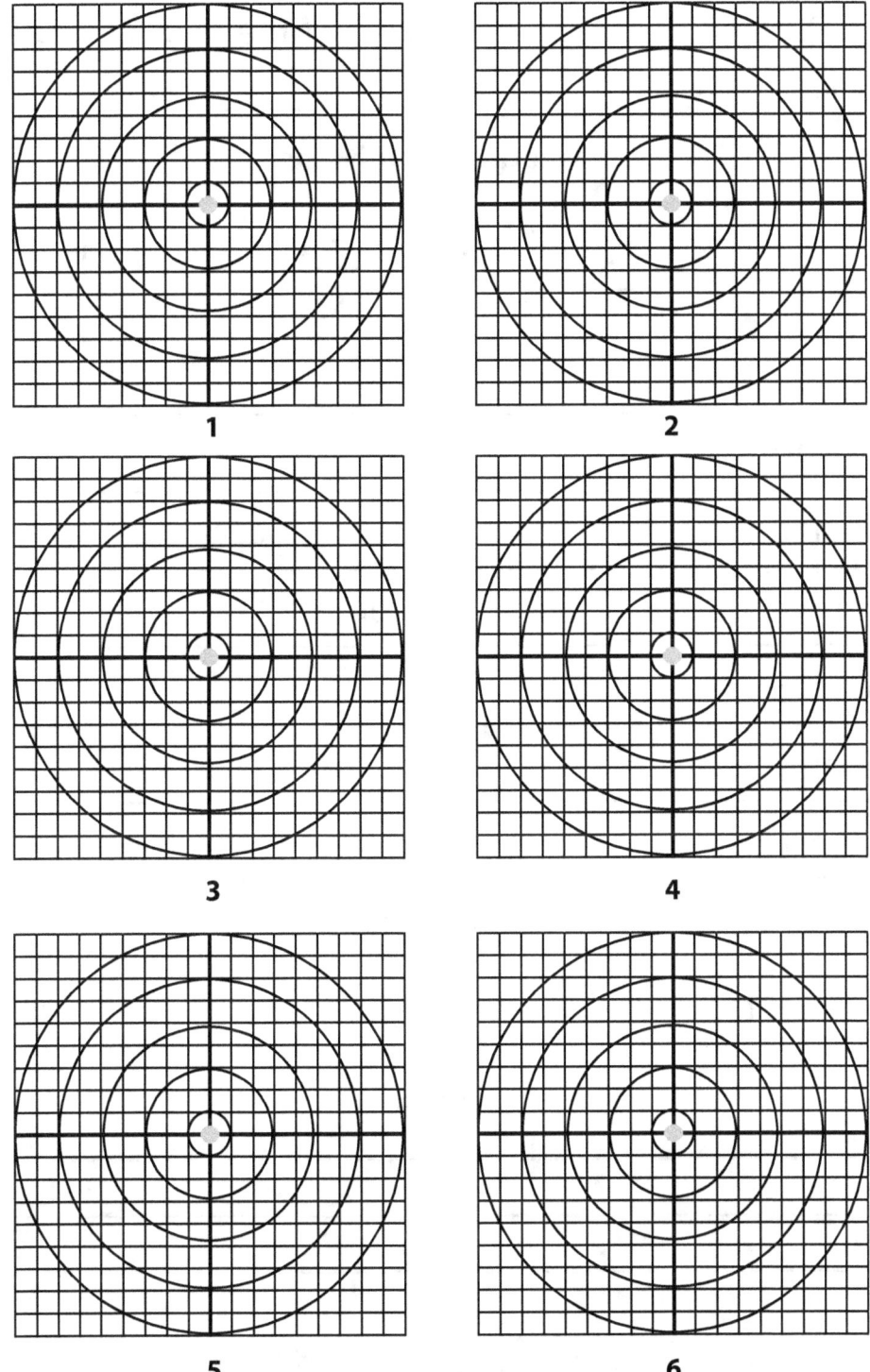

📅 Date: _____ 🕐 Time: _____

📍 Location: _____

Weather Conditions

☀️ ☐   ⛅ ☐   ☁️ ☐   🌧️ ☐   🌧️ ☐   🌨️ ☐   🚩 _____   🌡️ _____

Firearm:	
Bullet:	Seating Depth:
Powder:	Grains:
Primer:	
Brass:	
Distance:	

Overall Results

☐ Poor   ☐ Fair   ☐ Good   ☐ Excellent

Notes

_____

_____

_____

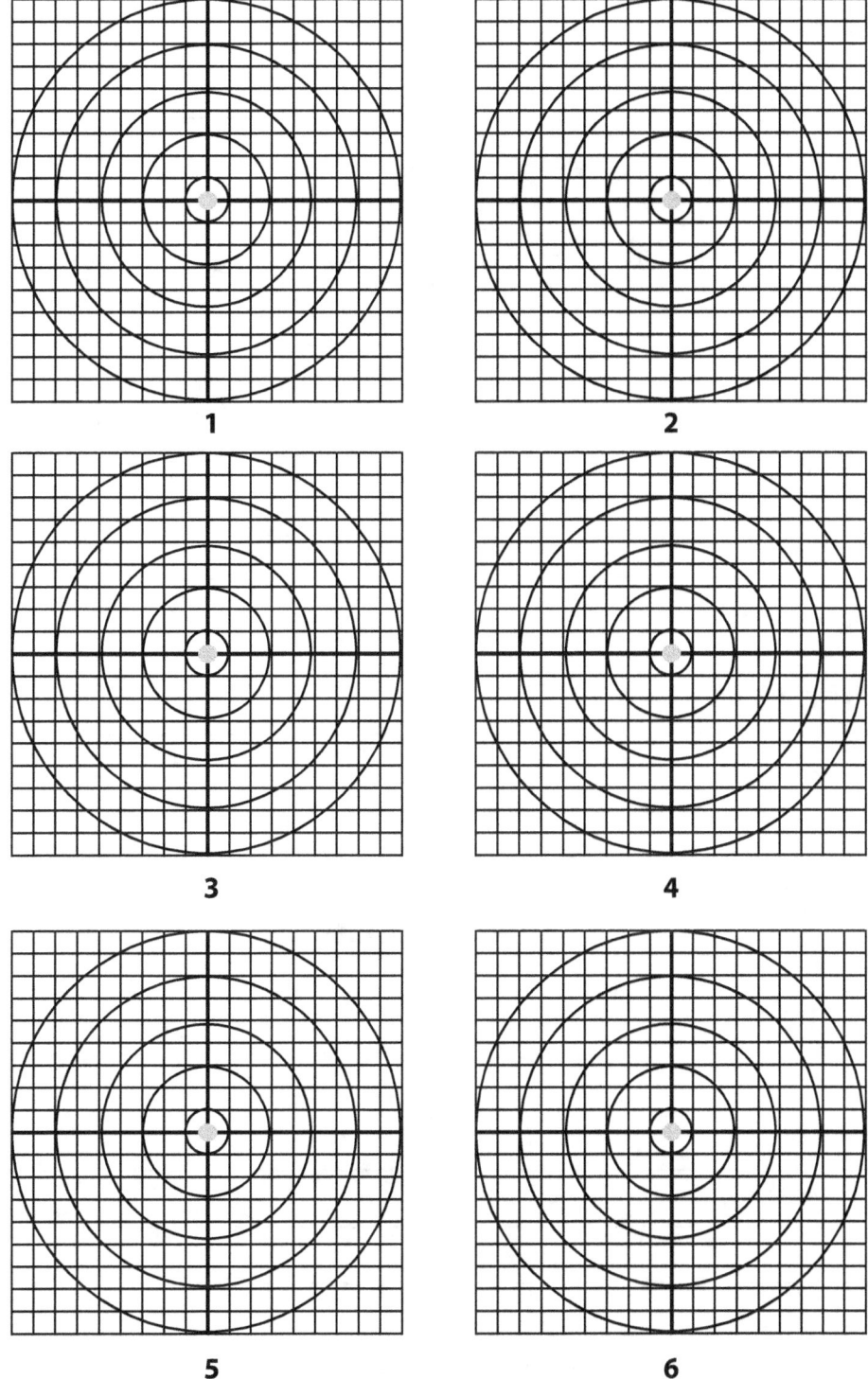

Date: _____ Time: _____

 Location: _____

Weather Conditions

☐ ☐ ☐ ☐ ☐ ☐ ____ ____

Firearm:	
Bullet:	Seating Depth:
Powder:	Grains:
Primer:	
Brass:	
Distance:	

Overall Results

☐ Poor   ☐ Fair   ☐ Good   ☐ Excellent

Notes

_____

_____

_____

☆ ☆ ☆ ☆ ☆

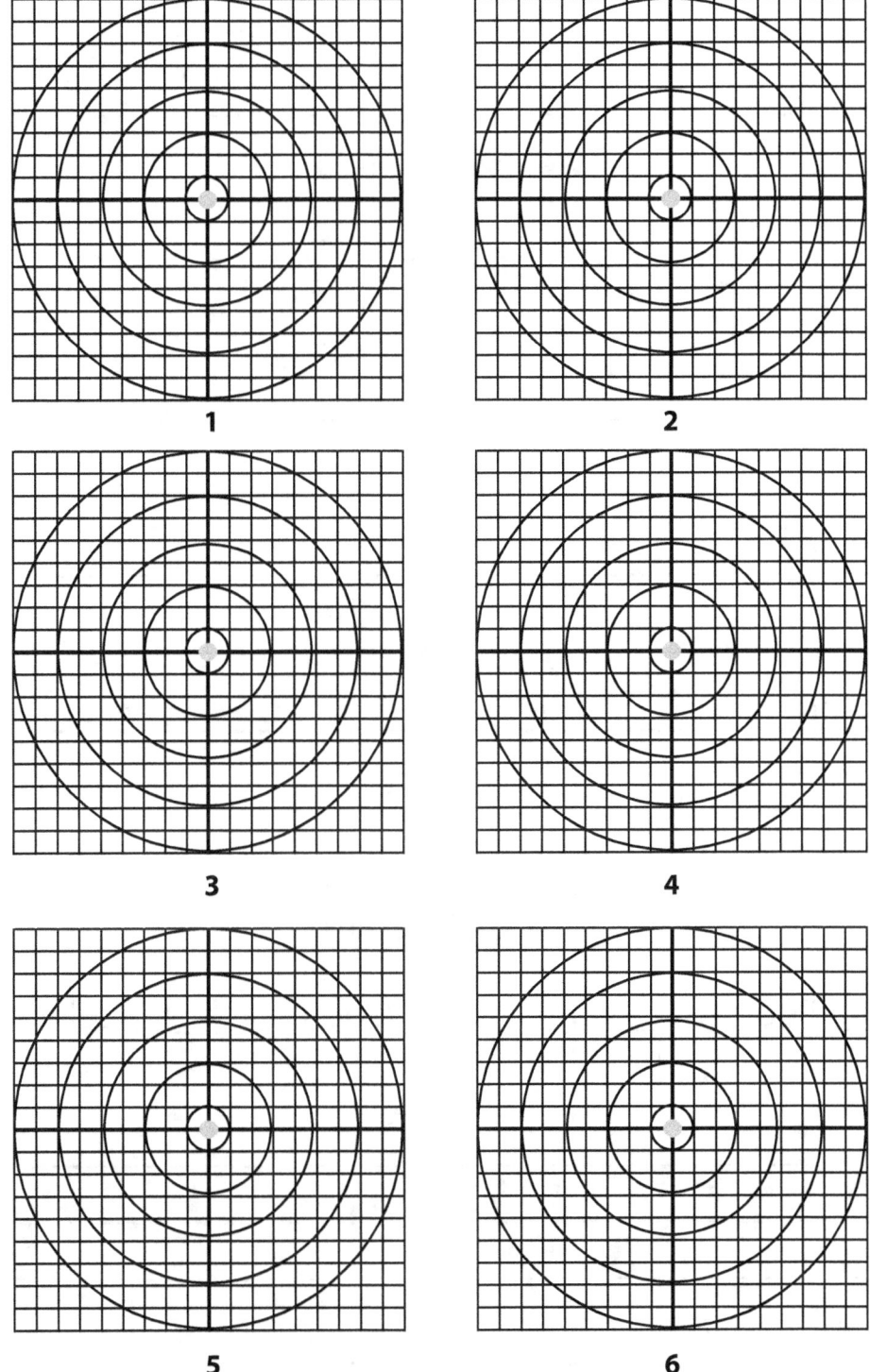

Date: _____ Time: _____

Location: _____

Weather Conditions

☀ ☁ 🌤 🌧 🌧 🌨 ⚑ 🌡
☐ ☐ ☐ ☐ ☐ ☐ _____ _____

Firearm:	
Bullet:	Seating Depth:
Powder:	Grains:
Primer:	
Brass:	
Distance:	

Overall Results

☐ Poor   ☐ Fair   ☐ Good   ☐ Excellent

Notes

_____

_____

☆ ☆ ☆ ☆ ☆

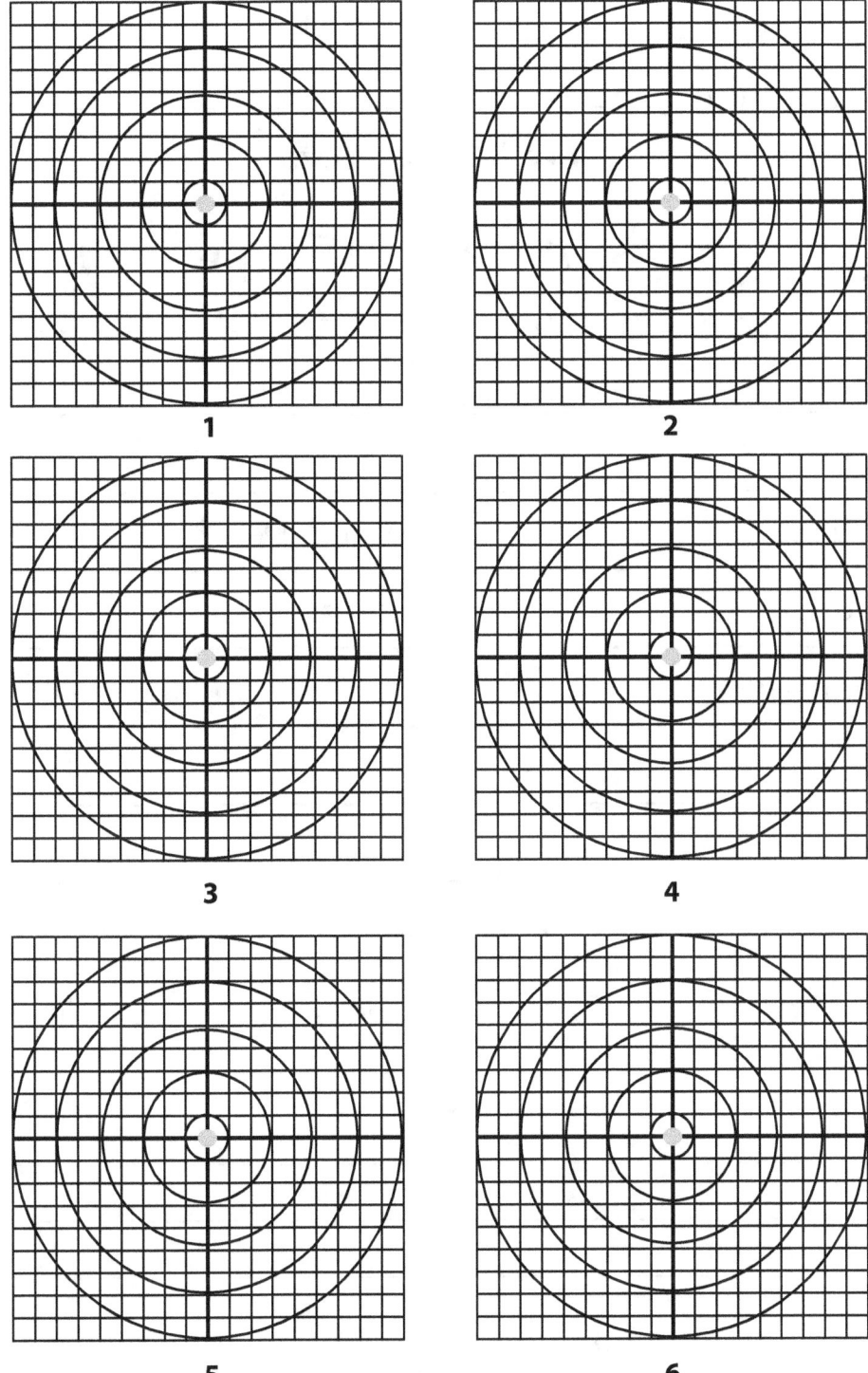

Date: _____ Time: _____

Location: _____

Weather Conditions

☀ ☁ ⛅ 🌧 🌧 🌨 ⛳ 🌡
☐ ☐ ☐ ☐ ☐ ☐ ____ ____

Firearm:	
Bullet:	Seating Depth:
Powder:	Grains:
Primer:	
Brass:	
Distance:	

Overall Results

☐ Poor   ☐ Fair   ☐ Good   ☐ Excellent

Notes

_____
_____
_____

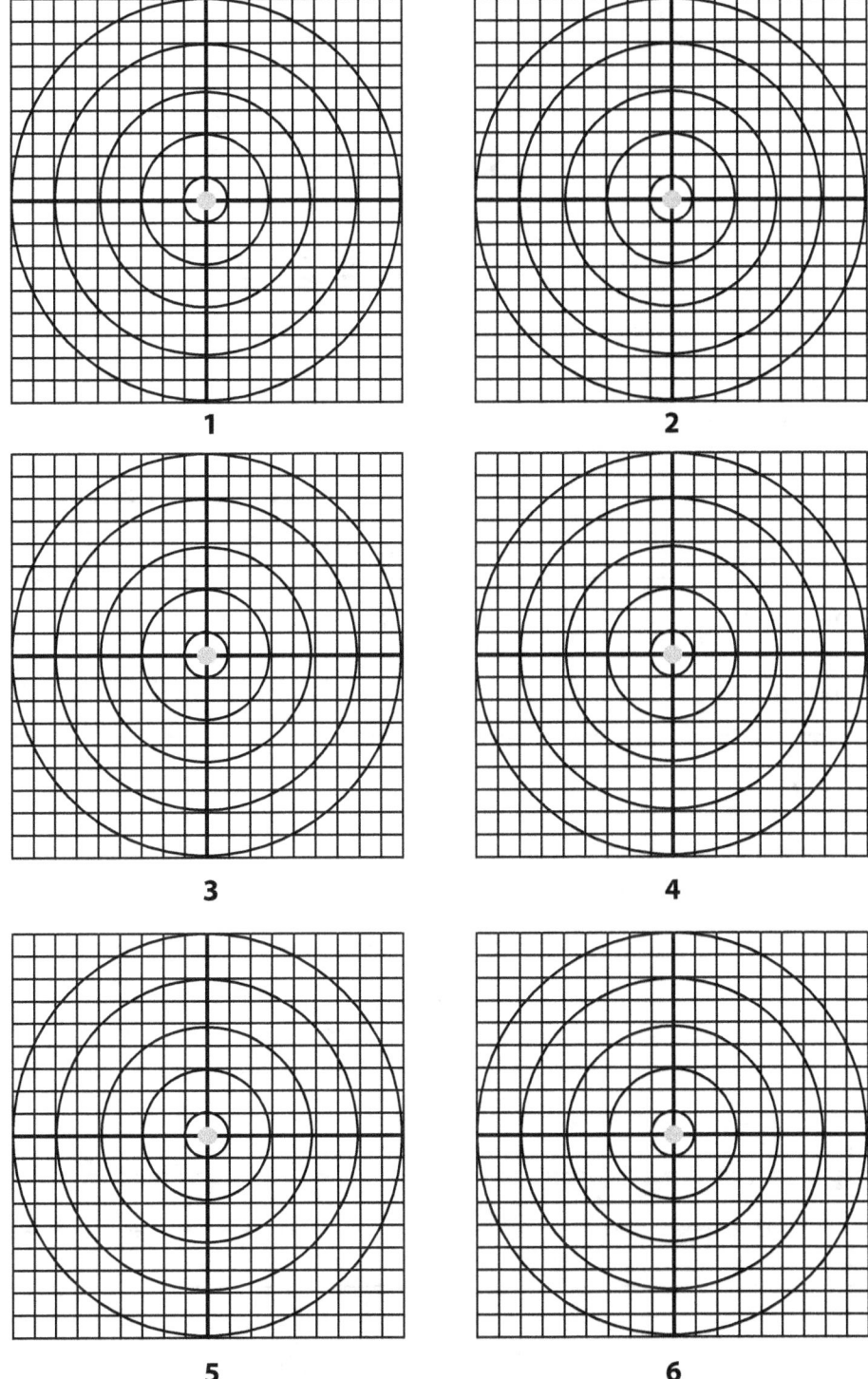

Date: _____ Time: _____

Location: _____

Weather Conditions

☀ ☁ ⛅ 🌧 🌧 🌨 🚩 🌡
☐ ☐ ☐ ☐ ☐ ☐ _____ _____

Firearm:	
Bullet:	Seating Depth:
Powder:	Grains:
Primer:	
Brass:	
Distance:	

Overall Results

☐ Poor   ☐ Fair   ☐ Good   ☐ Excellent

Notes

_____

_____

_____

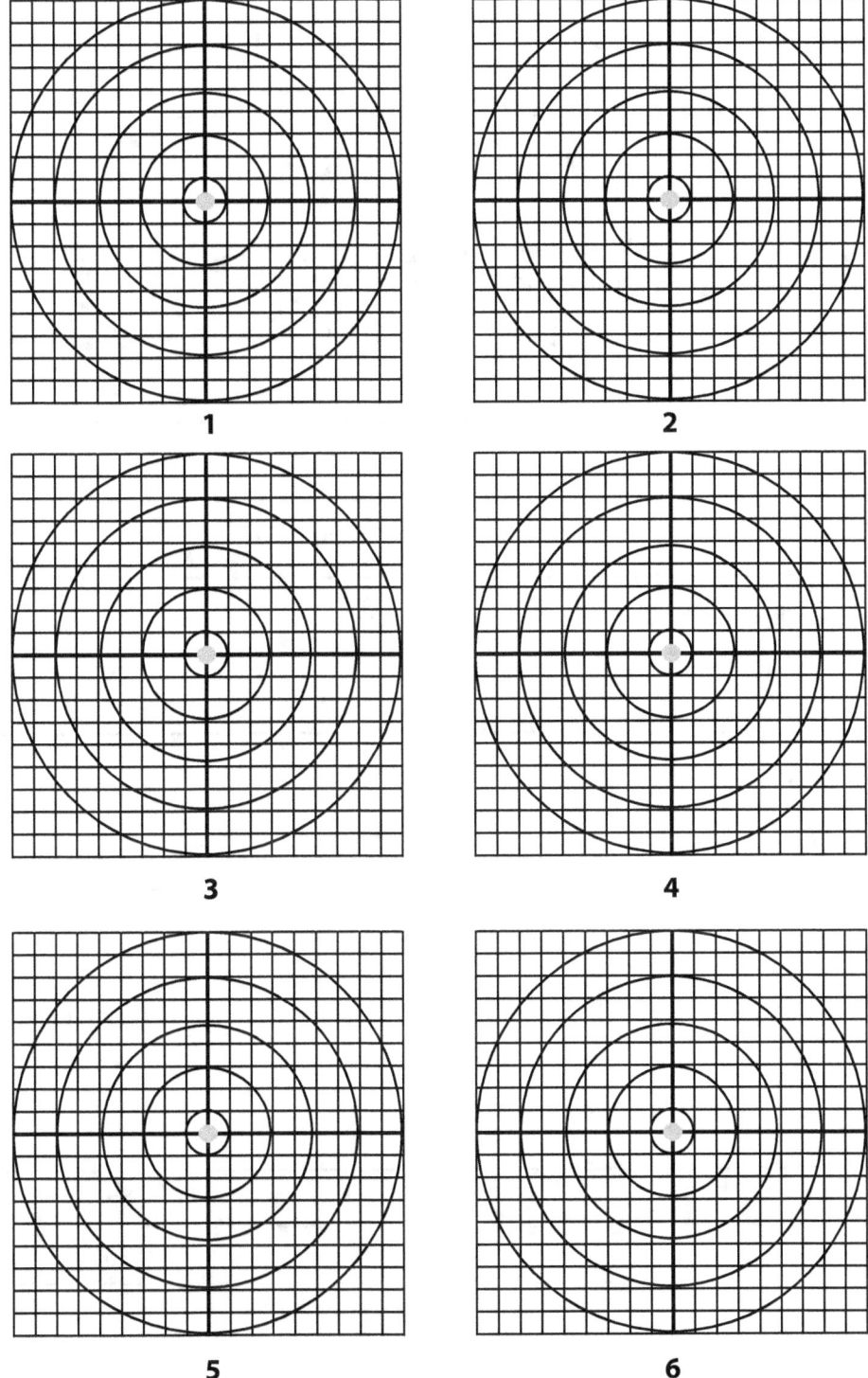

Date: _____ Time: _____

Location: _____

Weather Conditions

☐ ☐ ☐ ☐ ☐ ☐ _____ _____

Firearm:	
Bullet:	Seating Depth:
Powder:	Grains:
Primer:	
Brass:	
Distance:	

Overall Results

☐ Poor   ☐ Fair   ☐ Good   ☐ Excellent

Notes

_____

_____

_____

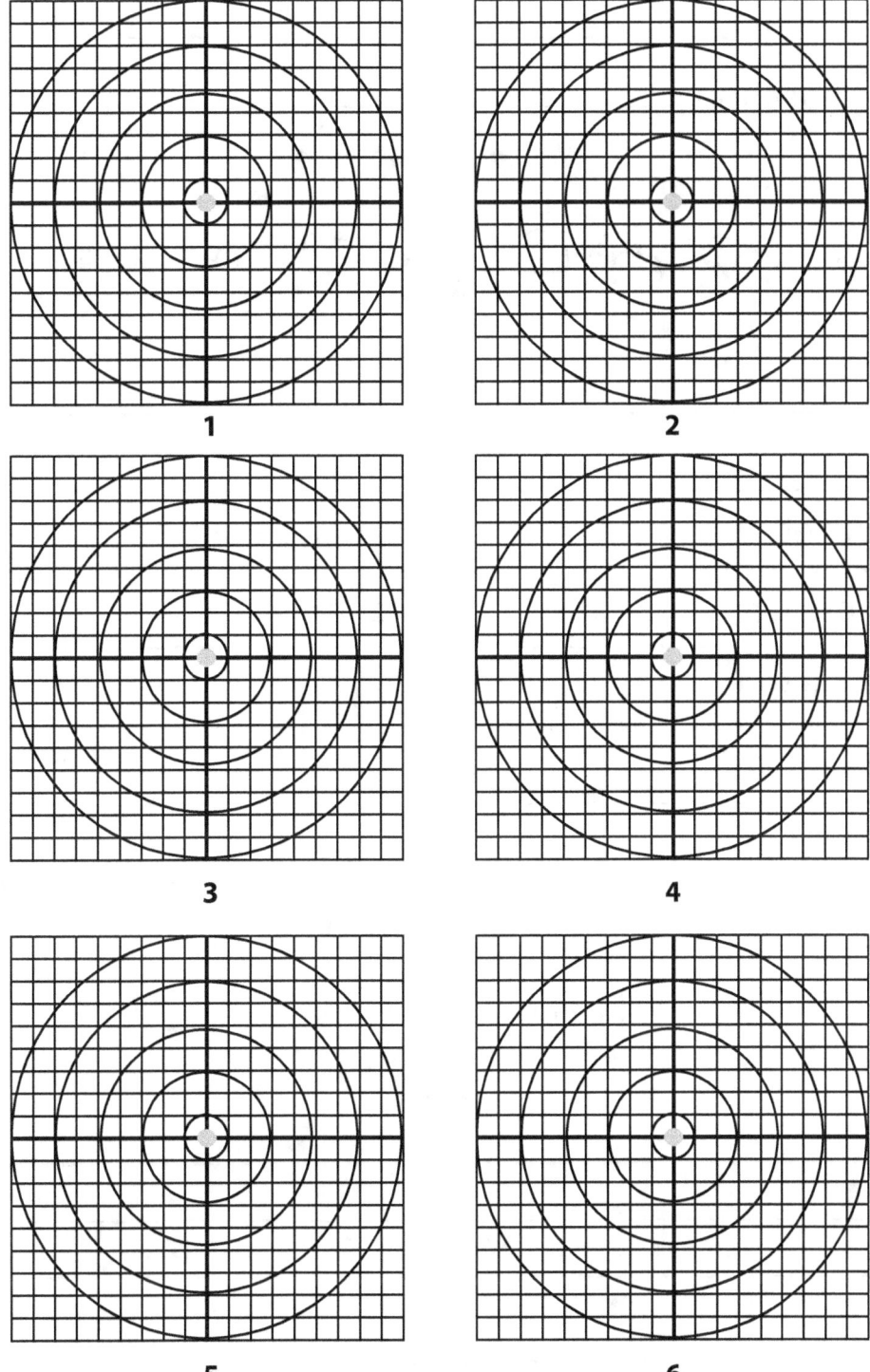

📅 Date: _____ 🕐 Time: _____

📍 Location: _____

Weather Conditions

☀️ ☐   ⛅ ☐   🌤 ☐   🌧 ☐   🌧 ☐   🌨 ☐   🚩 _____   🌡 _____

Firearm:	
Bullet:	Seating Depth:
Powder:	Grains:
Primer:	
Brass:	
Distance:	

Overall Results

☐ Poor   ☐ Fair   ☐ Good   ☐ Excellent

Notes

_____

_____

_____

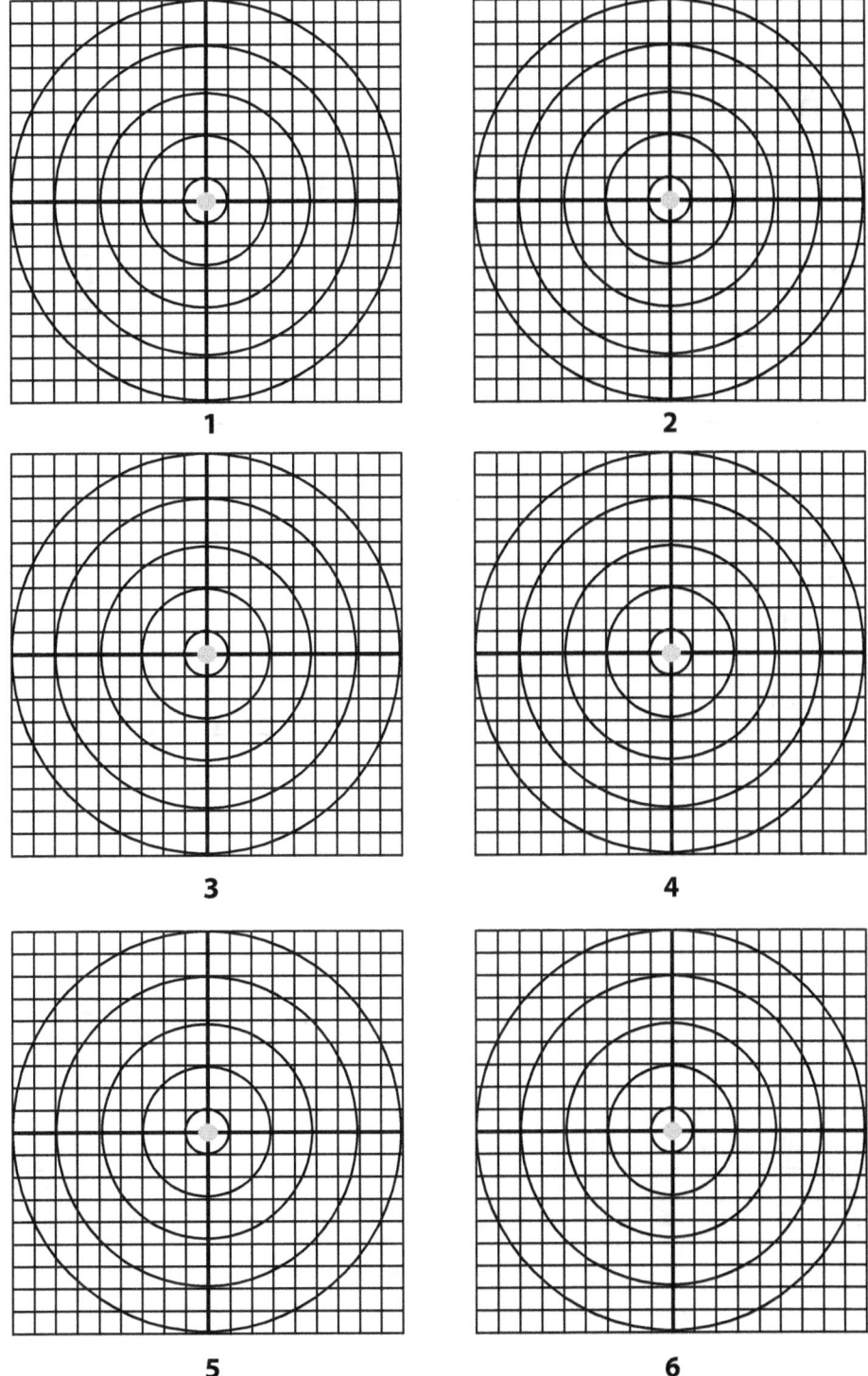

📅 Date: _____ 🕐 Time: _____

📍 Location: _____

Weather Conditions

☀️ ☁️ ⛅ 🌧️ 🌧️ 🌨️ 🚩 _____ 🌡️ _____
☐   ☐   ☐   ☐   ☐   ☐

Firearm:	
Bullet:	Seating Depth:
Powder:	Grains:
Primer:	
Brass:	
Distance:	

Overall Results

☐ Poor   ☐ Fair   ☐ Good   ☐ Excellent

Notes

_____

_____

_____

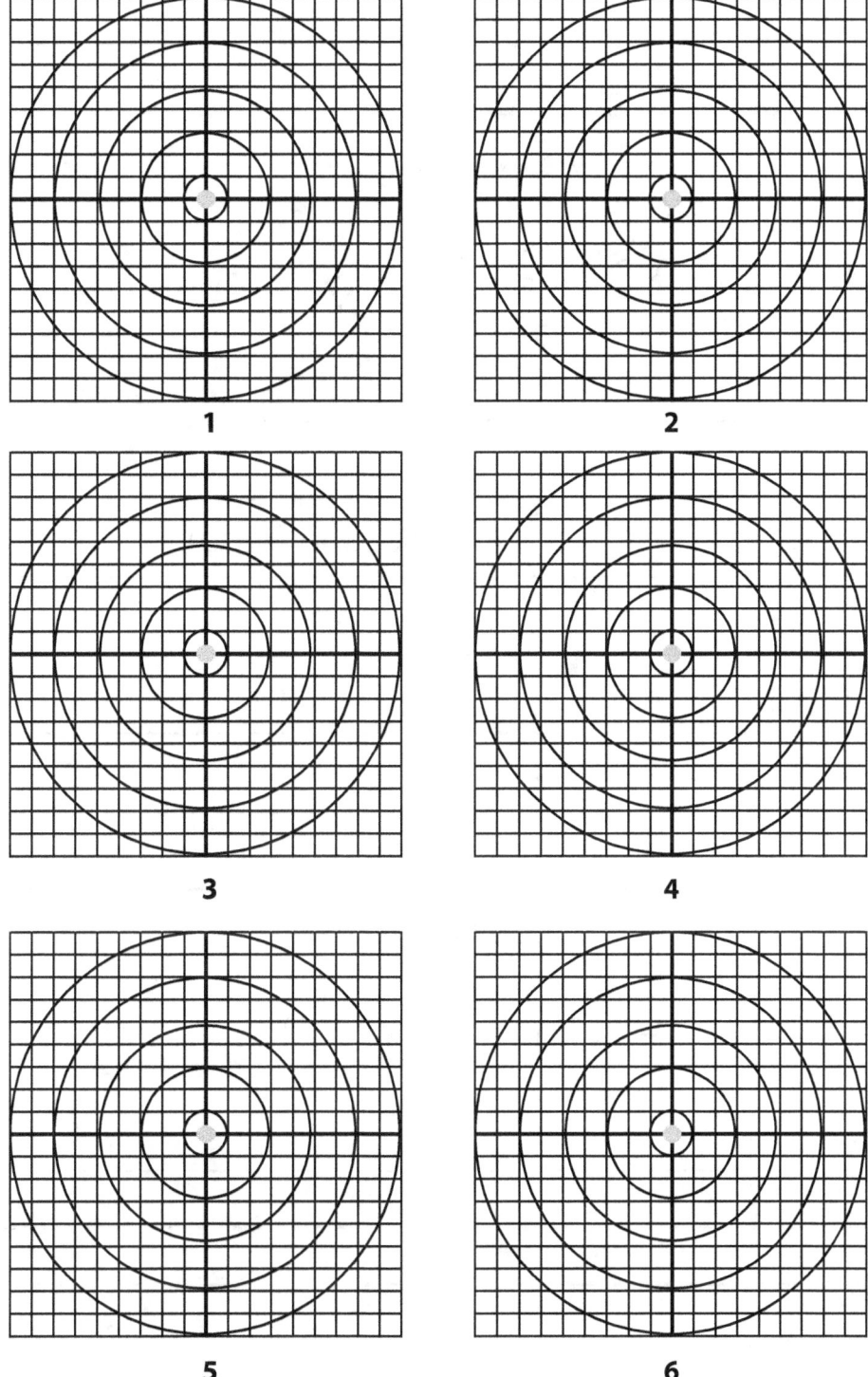

📅 Date: _____ 🕐 Time: _____

📍 Location: _____

Weather Conditions

☀ ☁ 🌤 🌧 🌦 🌨 ⚑ 🌡
☐ ☐ ☐ ☐ ☐ ☐ ___ ___

Firearm:	
Bullet:	Seating Depth:
Powder:	Grains:
Primer:	
Brass:	
Distance:	

Overall Results

☐ Poor   ☐ Fair   ☐ Good   ☐ Excellent

Notes

_____
_____
_____

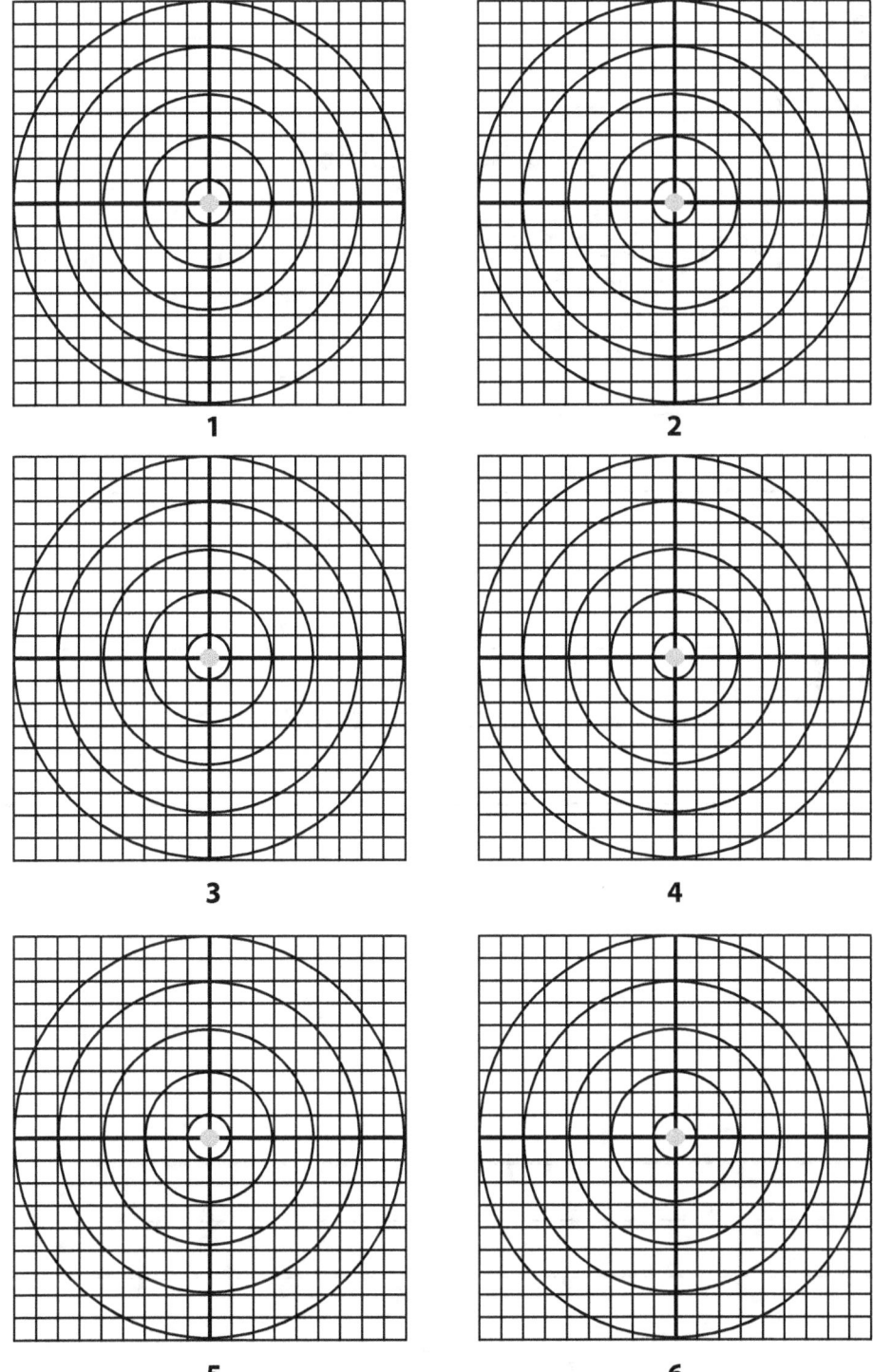

📅 Date: _____ 🕐 Time: _____

📍 Location: _____

Weather Conditions

☀ ☐   ⛅ ☐   🌤 ☐   🌧 ☐   🌧 ☐   🌨 ☐   🚩 _____   🌡 _____

Firearm:	
Bullet:	Seating Depth:
Powder:	Grains:
Primer:	
Brass:	
Distance:	

Overall Results

☐ Poor   ☐ Fair   ☐ Good   ☐ Excellent

Notes

_____

_____

_____

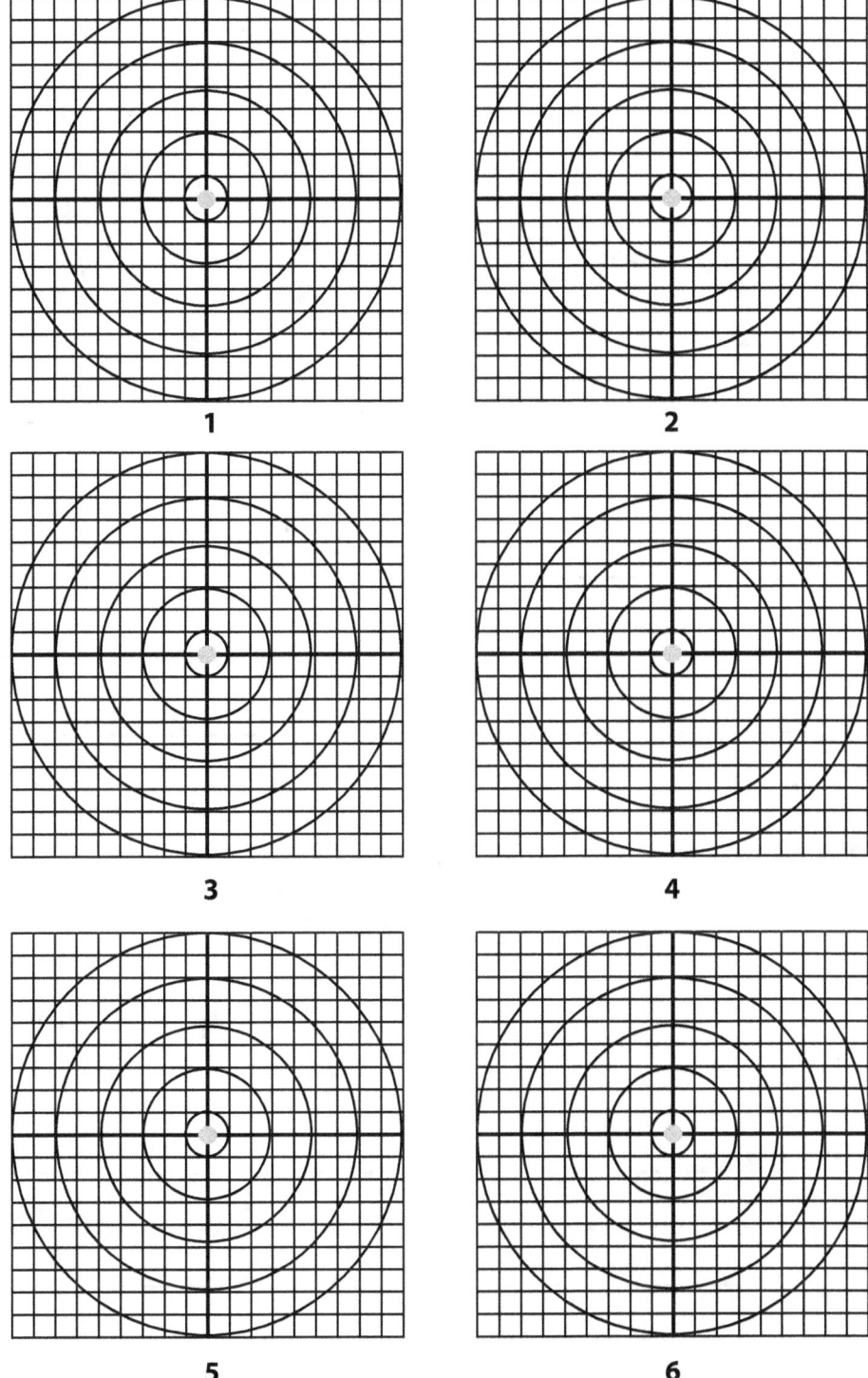

Date: _____ Time: _____

 Location: _____

Weather Conditions

☀ ☁ ⛅ 🌧 🌧 🌨 🚩 🌡
☐ ☐ ☐ ☐ ☐ ☐ ___ ___

Firearm:	
Bullet:	Seating Depth:
Powder:	Grains:
Primer:	
Brass:	
Distance:	

Overall Results

☐ Poor   ☐ Fair   ☐ Good   ☐ Excellent

Notes

_____

_____

_____

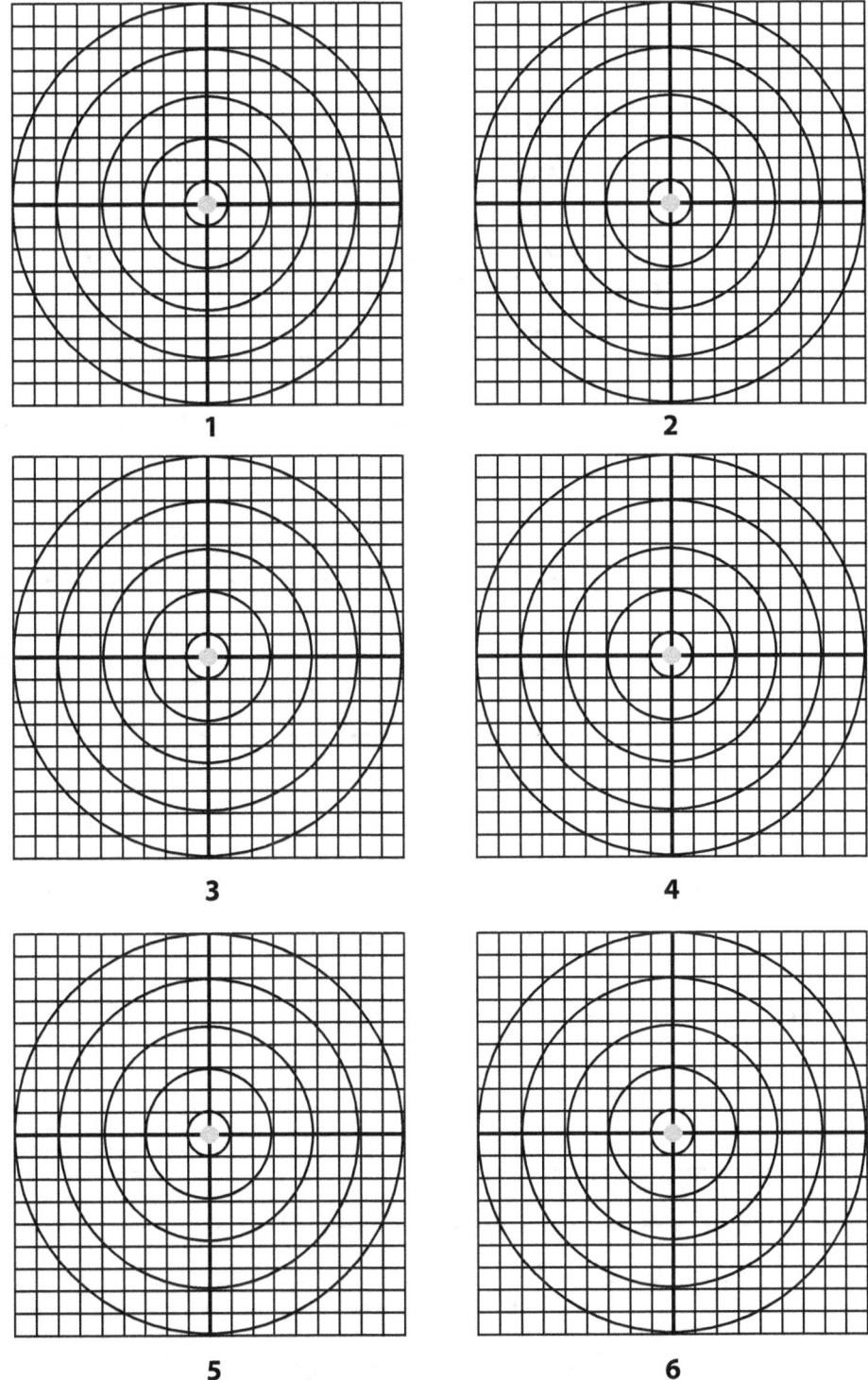

Date: _____ Time: _____

Location: _____

Weather Conditions

☀ ☁ ⛅ ☁ 🌧 🌧 🚩 🌡
☐ ☐ ☐ ☐ ☐ ☐

Firearm:	
Bullet:	Seating Depth:
Powder:	Grains:
Primer:	
Brass:	
Distance:	

Overall Results

☐ Poor   ☐ Fair   ☐ Good   ☐ Excellent

Notes

_____

_____

_____

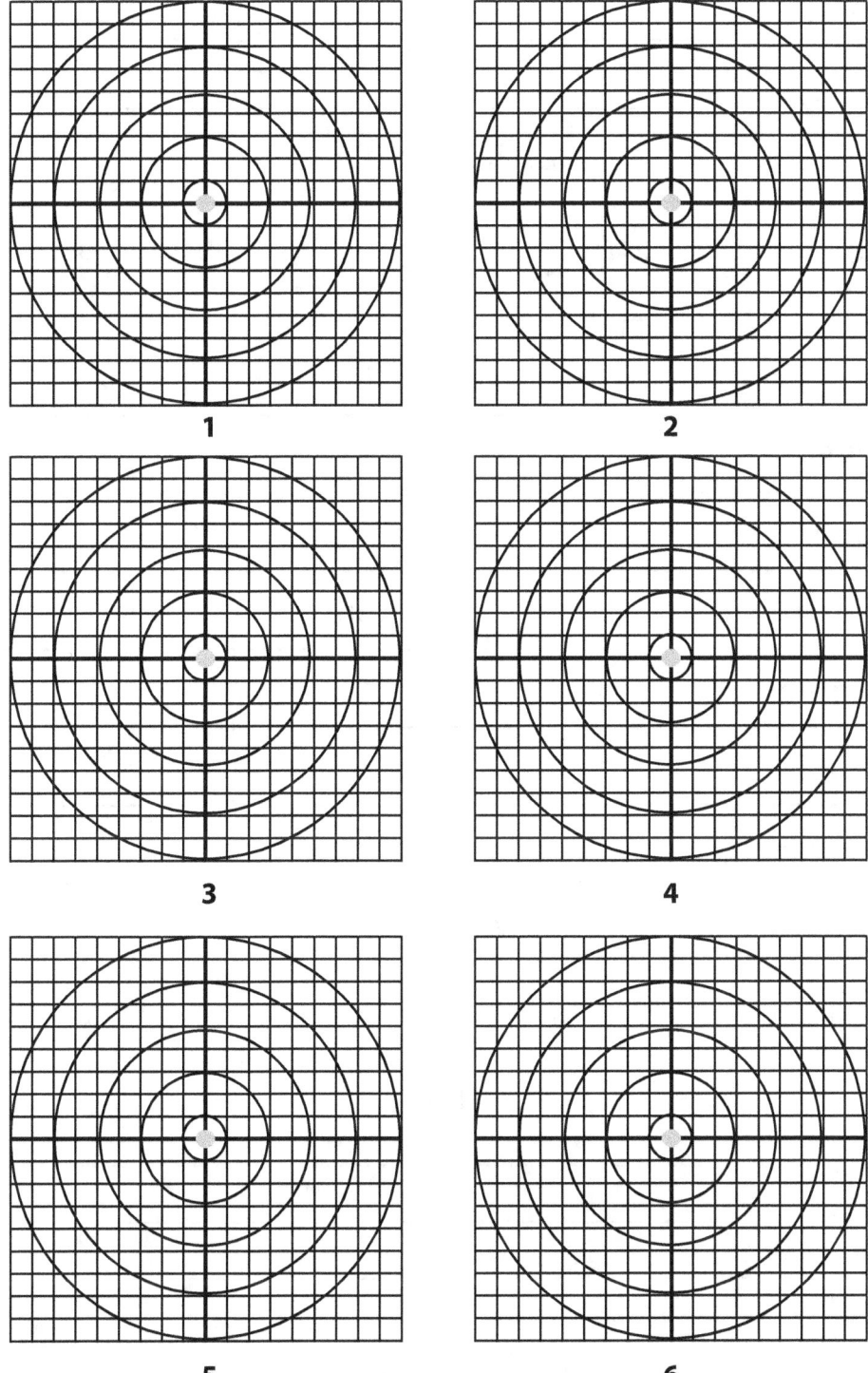

📅 Date: _____   🕐 Time: _____

📍 Location: _____

Weather Conditions

☀ ☁ 🌤 🌧 🌧 🌨 ⚑ 🌡
☐ ☐ ☐ ☐ ☐ ☐ ____ ____

Firearm:	
Bullet:	Seating Depth:
Powder:	Grains:
Primer:	
Brass:	
Distance:	

Overall Results

☐ Poor   ☐ Fair   ☐ Good   ☐ Excellent

Notes

_____
_____
_____

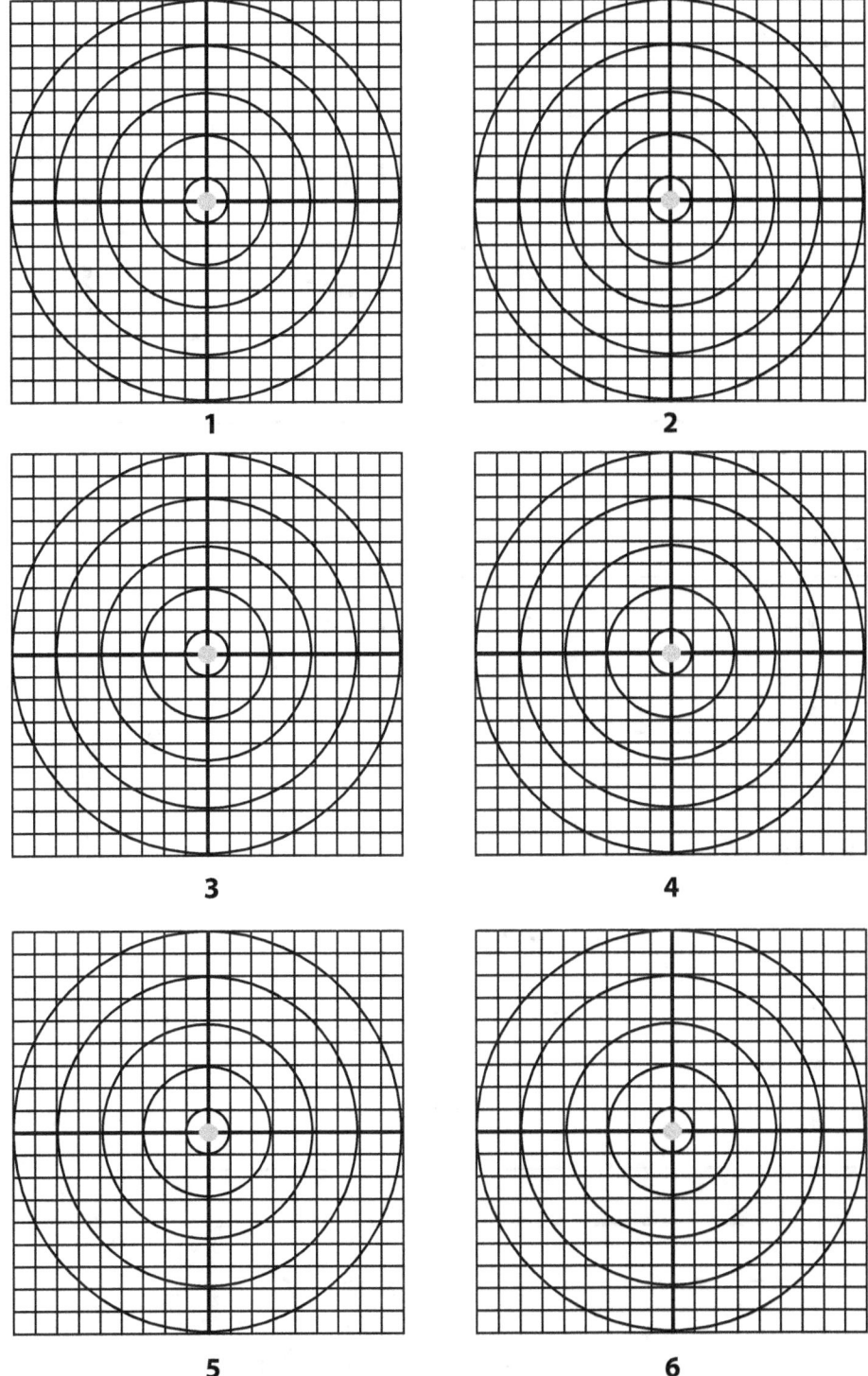

Date: _____ Time: _____

 Location: _____

Weather Conditions

☀ ☁ ⛅ 🌧 🌦 🌨 🚩 🌡
☐   ☐   ☐   ☐   ☐   ☐   ____   ____

Firearm:	
Bullet:	Seating Depth:
Powder:	Grains:
Primer:	
Brass:	
Distance:	

Overall Results

☐ Poor   ☐ Fair   ☐ Good   ☐ Excellent

Notes

_____

_____

_____

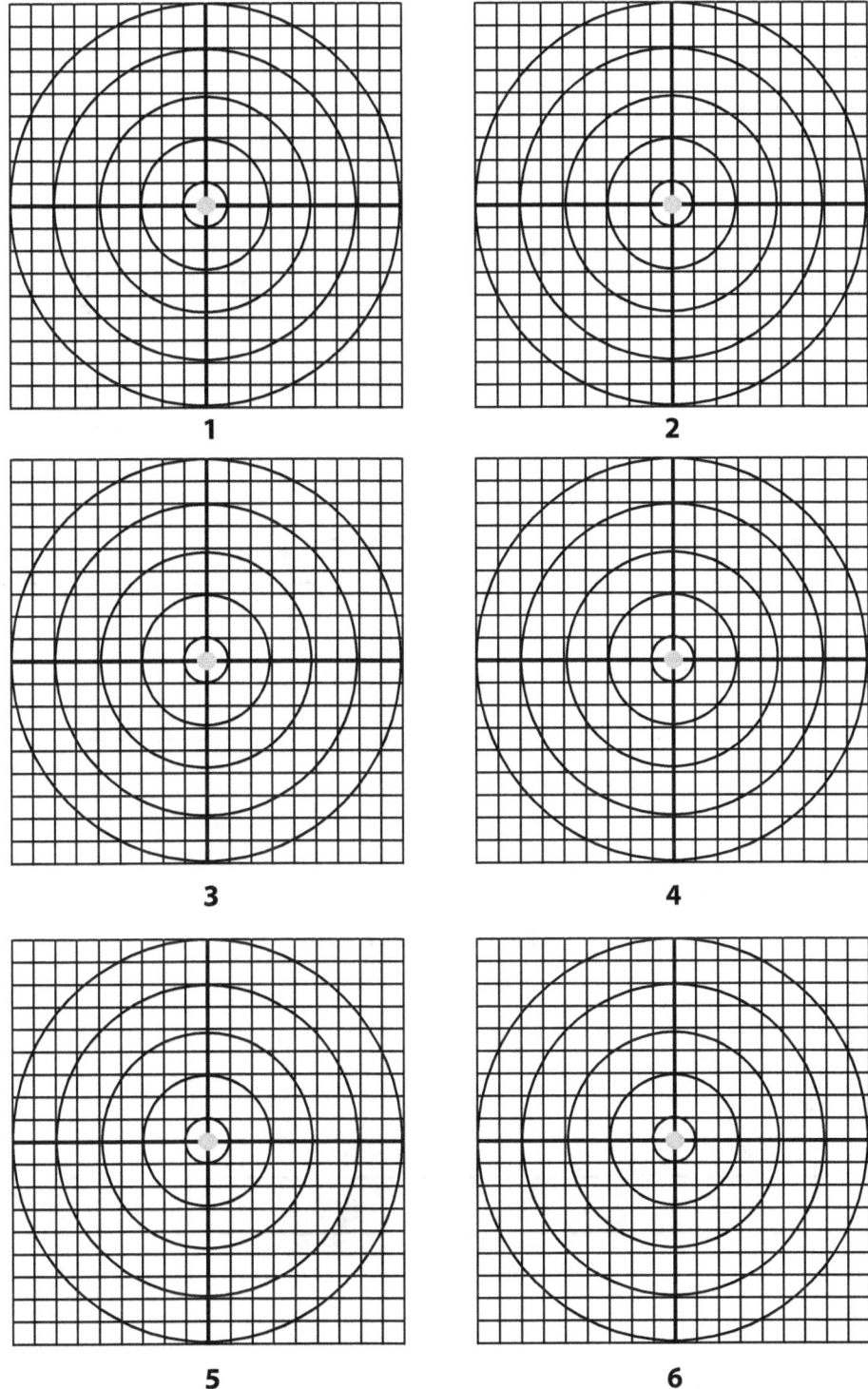

📅 Date: _____   🕐 Time: _____

📍 Location: _____

Weather Conditions

☀ ☁ 🌤 🌧 🌧 🌨 🚩 🌡
☐ ☐ ☐ ☐ ☐ ☐ ___ ___

Firearm:	
Bullet:	Seating Depth:
Powder:	Grains:
Primer:	
Brass:	
Distance:	

Overall Results

☐ Poor   ☐ Fair   ☐ Good   ☐ Excellent

Notes

_____

_____

_____

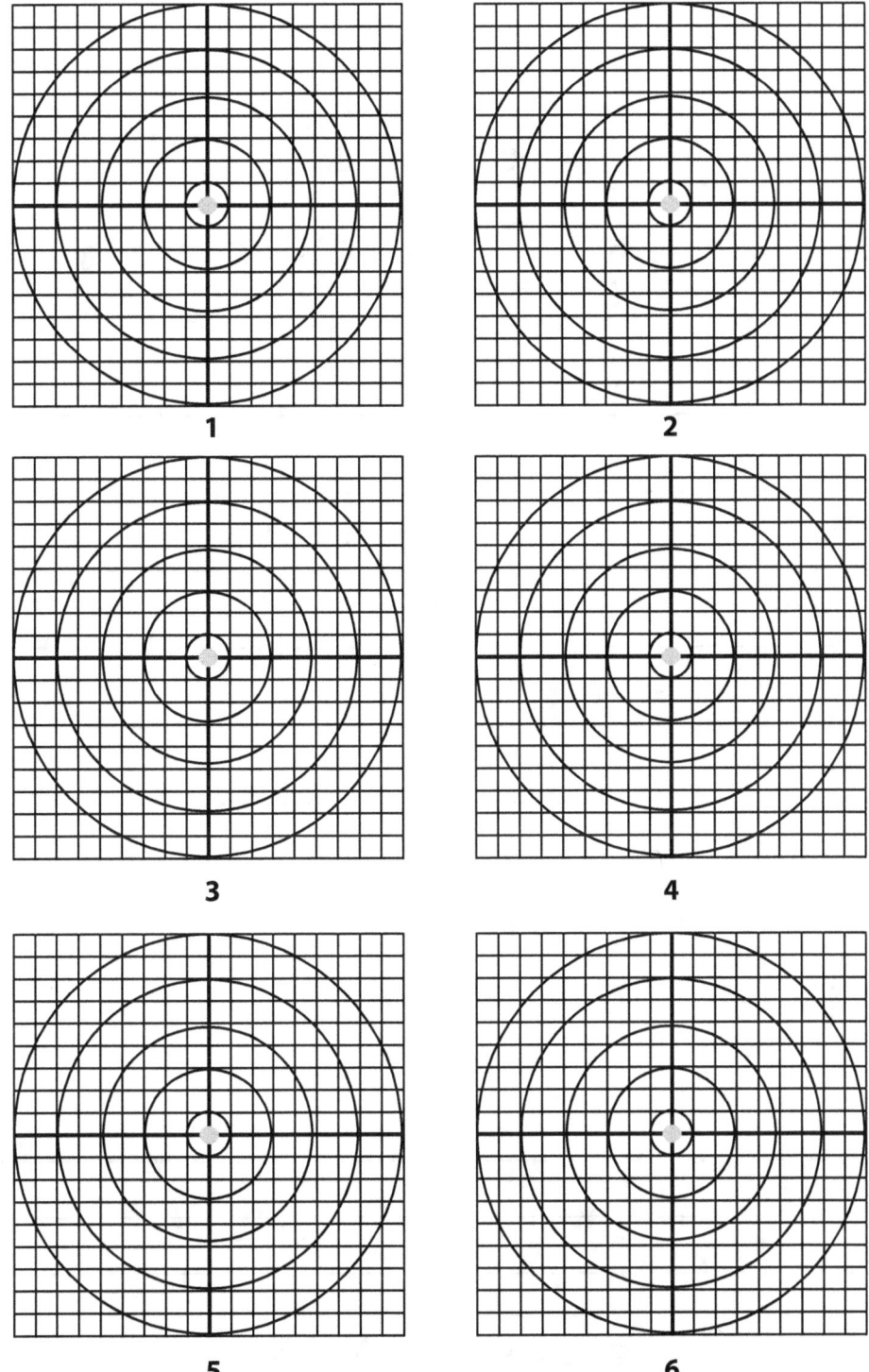

Date: _____ Time: _____
 Location: _____

Weather Conditions

☀ ☁ ⛅ 🌧 🌧 🌨 🚩 🌡
☐ ☐ ☐ ☐ ☐ ☐ ___ ___

Firearm:	
Bullet:	Seating Depth:
Powder:	Grains:
Primer:	
Brass:	
Distance:	

Overall Results

☐ Poor   ☐ Fair   ☐ Good   ☐ Excellent

Notes

_____
_____
_____

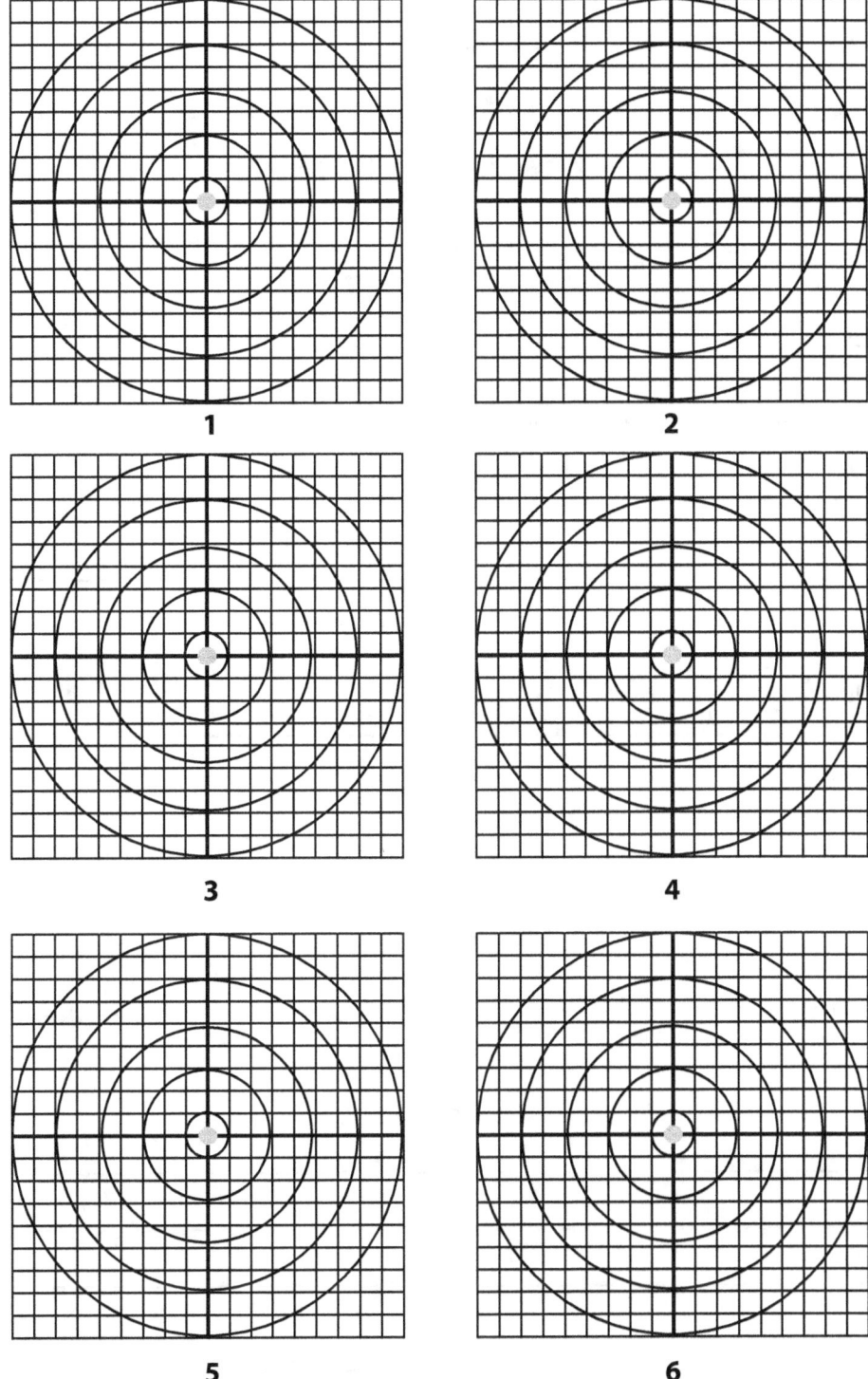

Date: _____   Time: _____

Location: _____

Weather Conditions

☐ ☐ ☐ ☐ ☐ ☐   _____   _____

Firearm:	
Bullet:	Seating Depth:
Powder:	Grains:
Primer:	
Brass:	
Distance:	

Overall Results

☐ Poor   ☐ Fair   ☐ Good   ☐ Excellent

Notes

_____

_____

_____

☆ ☆ ☆ ☆ ☆

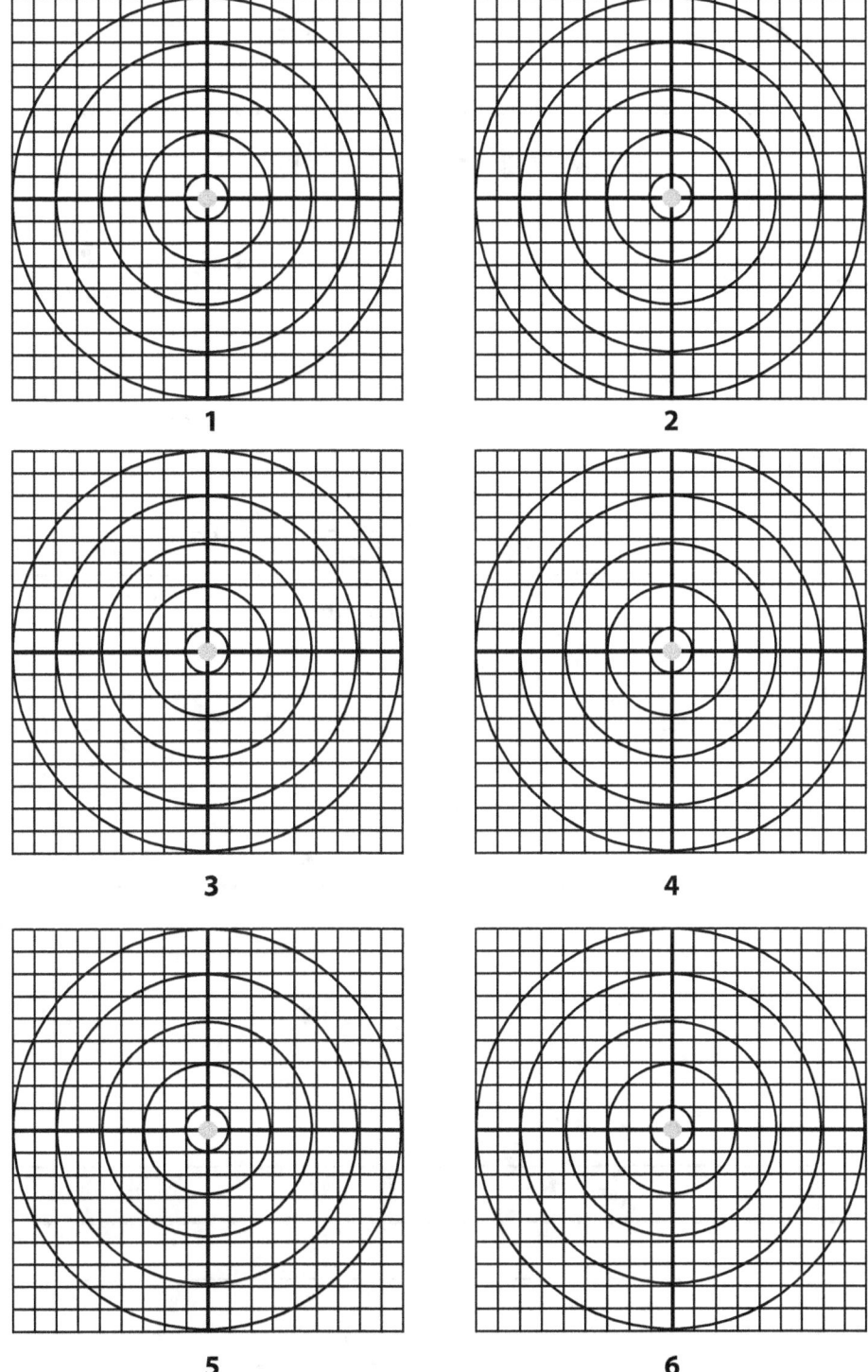

Date: _____   Time: _____

Location: _____

Weather Conditions

☀ ☁ ⛅ 🌧 🌧 🌨 🚩 🌡
☐ ☐ ☐ ☐ ☐ ☐ ___ ___

Firearm:	
Bullet:	Seating Depth:
Powder:	Grains:
Primer:	
Brass:	
Distance:	

Overall Results

☐ Poor   ☐ Fair   ☐ Good   ☐ Excellent

Notes

_____
_____
_____

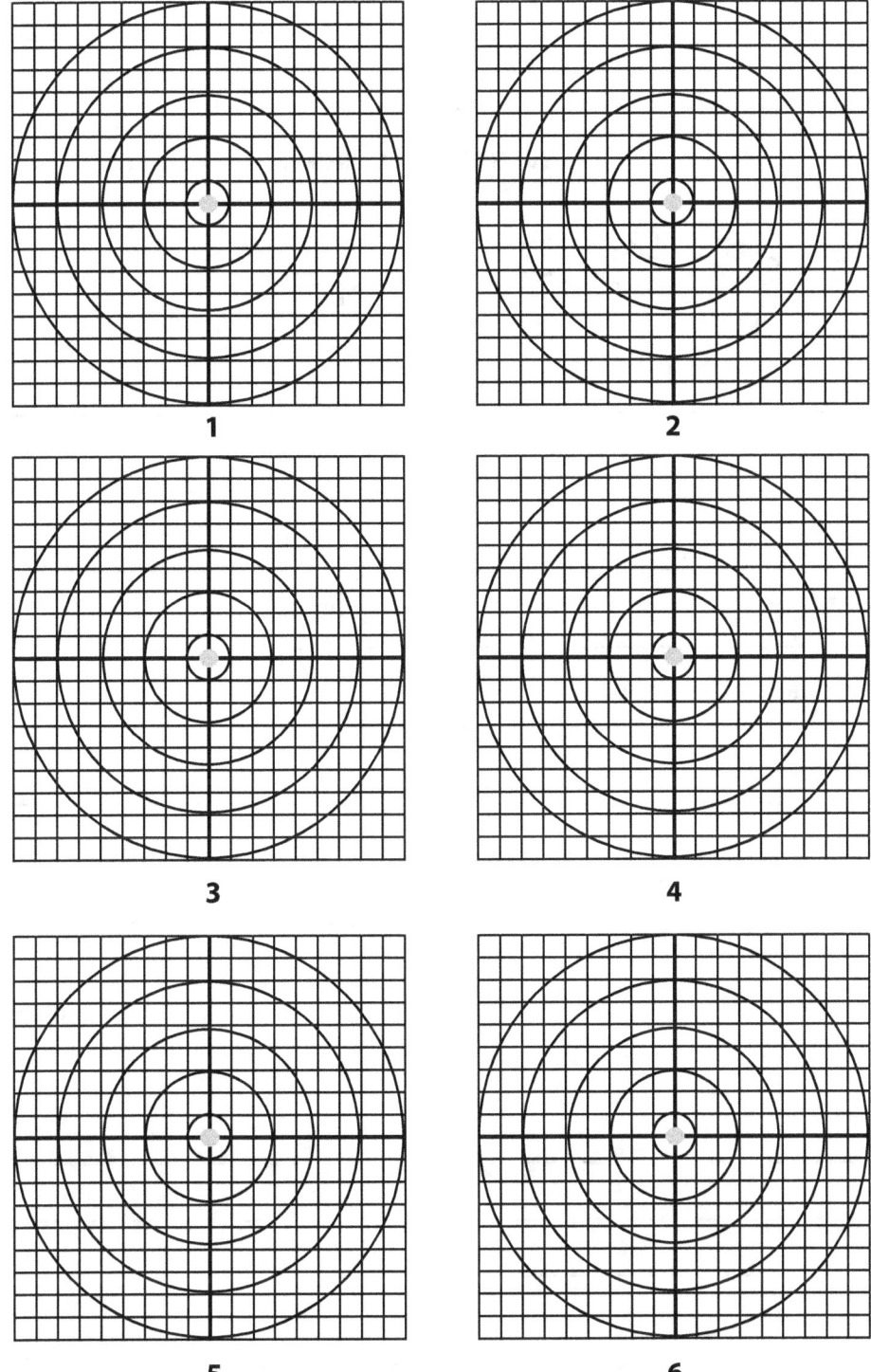

Date: _____ **Time:** _____

Location: _____

Weather Conditions

☀️ ☐ ⛅ ☐ ☁️ ☐ 🌧️ ☐ 🌧️ ☐ 🌨️ ☐ 🚩 _____ 🌡️ _____

Firearm:	
Bullet:	Seating Depth:
Powder:	Grains:
Primer:	
Brass:	
Distance:	

Overall Results

☐ Poor   ☐ Fair   ☐ Good   ☐ Excellent

Notes

_____

_____

_____

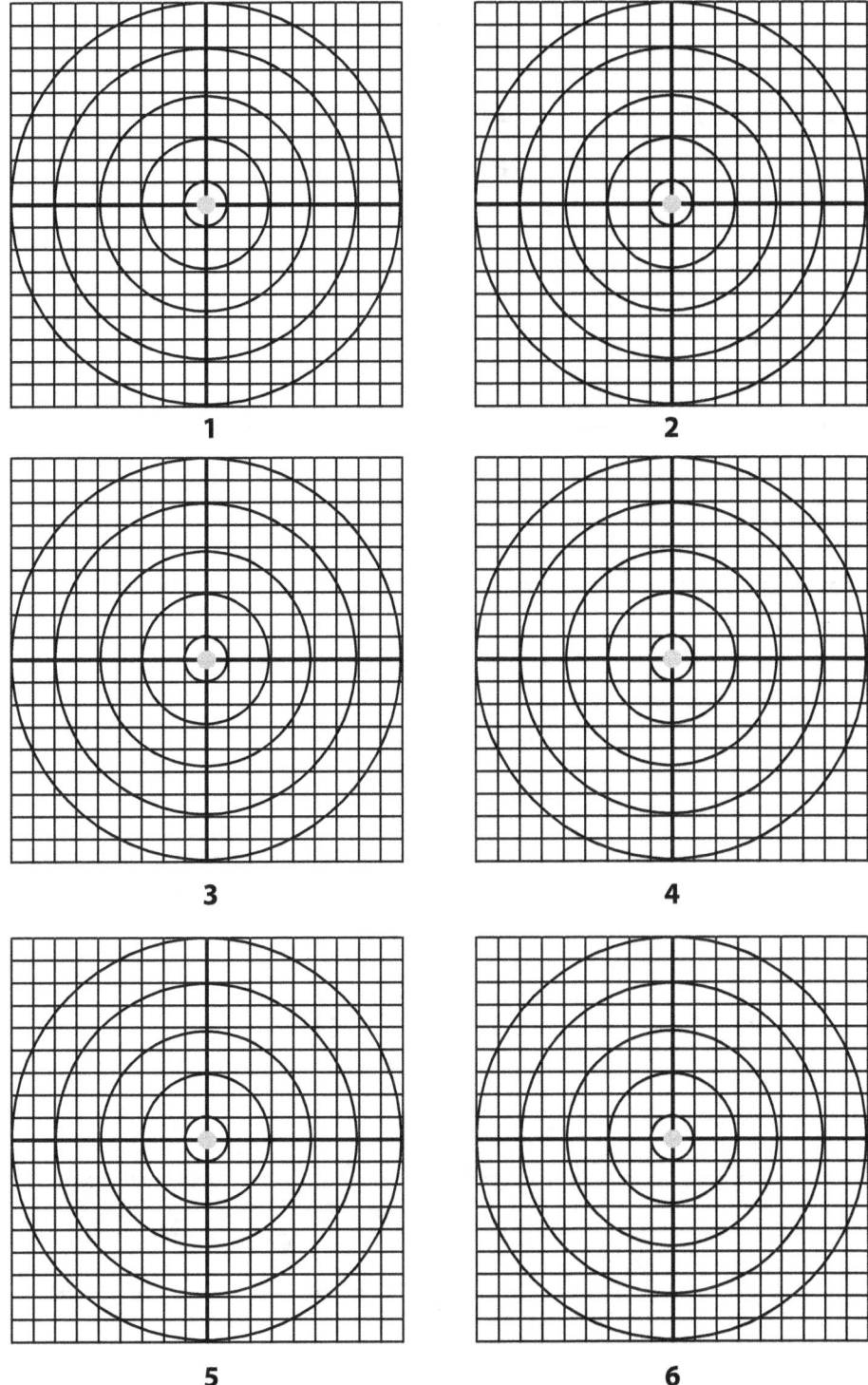

Date: _____ Time: _____
 Location: _____

Weather Conditions

☀ ☁ ⛅ 🌧 🌧 🌨 🚩 🌡
☐ ☐ ☐ ☐ ☐ ☐ ___ ___

Firearm:	
Bullet:	Seating Depth:
Powder:	Grains:
Primer:	
Brass:	
Distance:	

Overall Results

☐ Poor ☐ Fair ☐ Good ☐ Excellent

Notes

_____
_____
_____

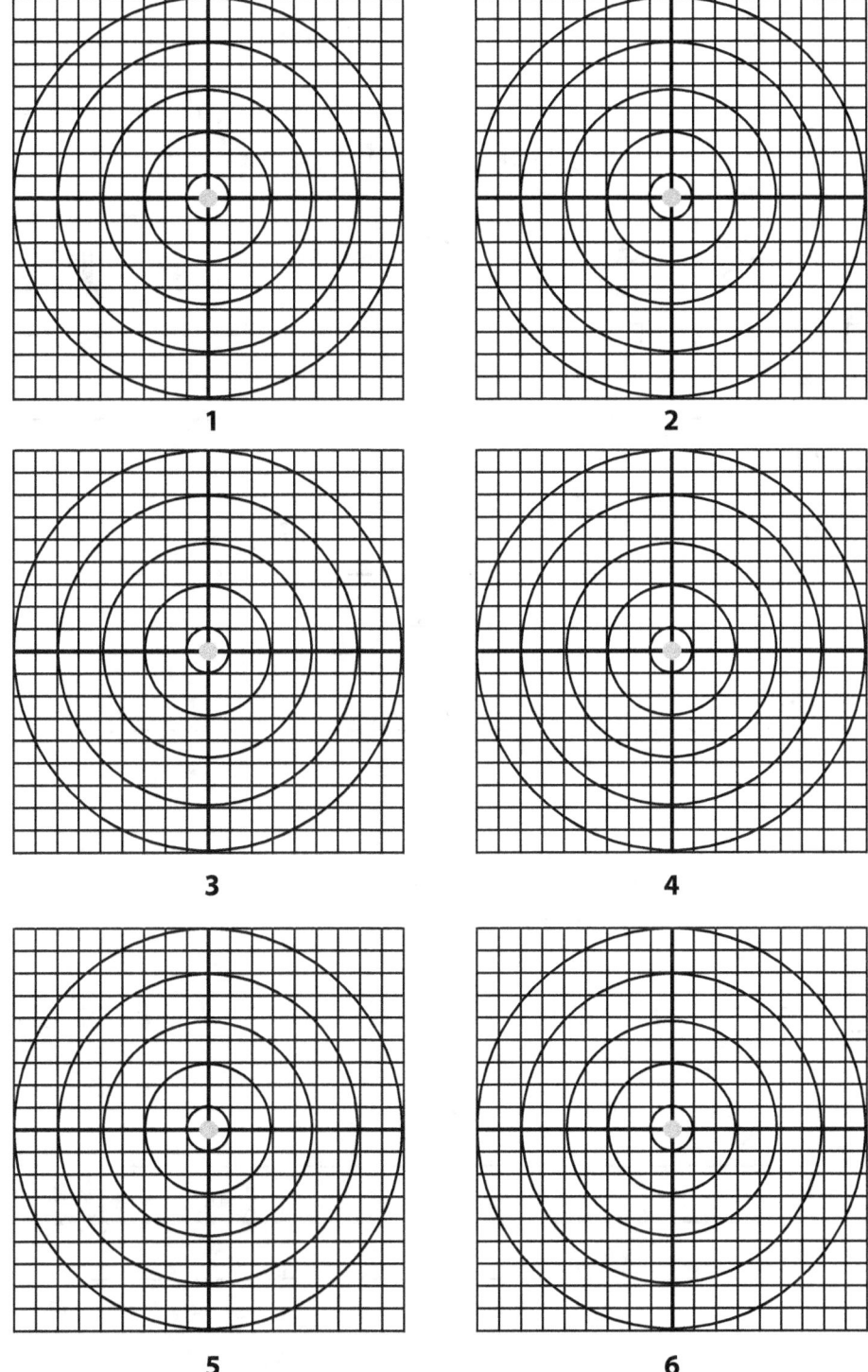

📅 Date: _____ 🕐 Time: _____

📍 Location: _____

Weather Conditions

☀️ ☁️ 🌤️ 🌧️ 🌧️ 🌨️ 🚩_____ 🌡️_____
☐   ☐   ☐   ☐   ☐   ☐

Firearm:	
Bullet:	Seating Depth:
Powder:	Grains:
Primer:	
Brass:	
Distance:	

Overall Results

☐ Poor   ☐ Fair   ☐ Good   ☐ Excellent

Notes

_____

_____

_____

☆ ☆ ☆ ☆ ☆

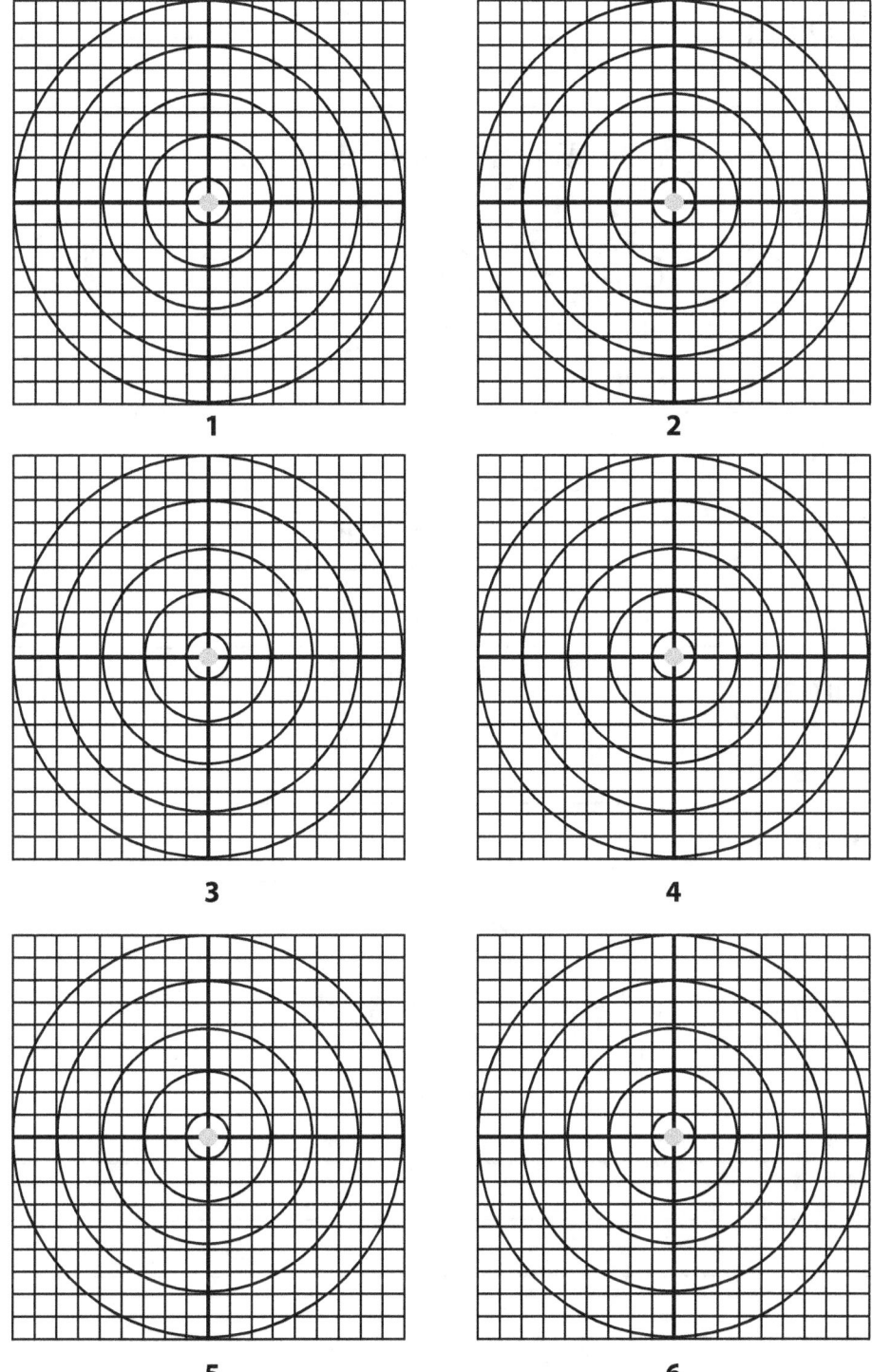

Date: _____ 🕐 Time: _____

📍 Location: _____

Weather Conditions

☀️ ☁️ 🌤 ☁️ 🌧 🌨 🚩 🌡
☐   ☐   ☐   ☐   ☐   ☐   _____   _____

Firearm:	
Bullet:	Seating Depth:
Powder:	Grains:
Primer:	
Brass:	
Distance:	

Overall Results

☐ Poor   ☐ Fair   ☐ Good   ☐ Excellent

Notes

_____
_____
_____

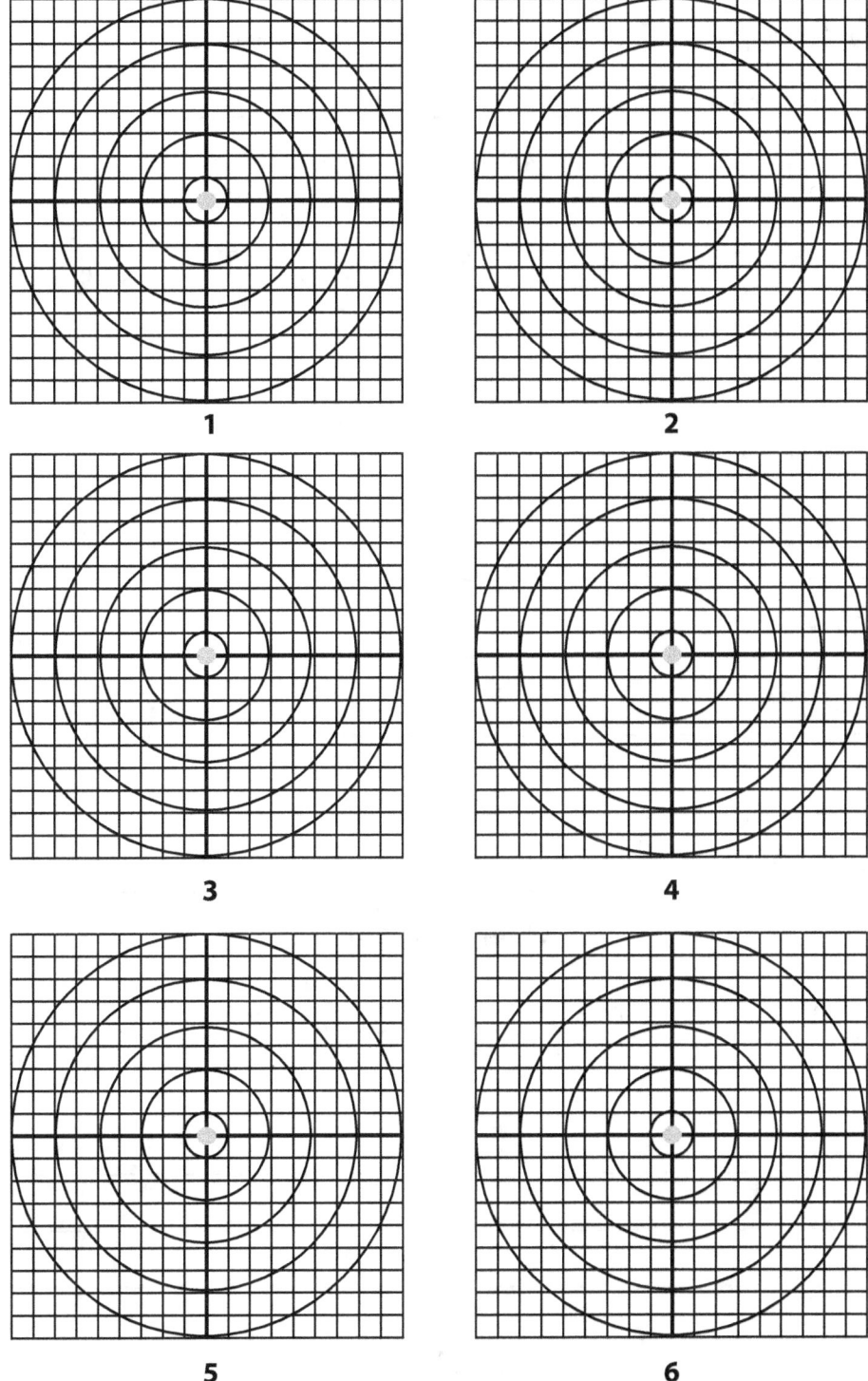

📅 Date: _____ 🕐 Time: _____

📍 Location: _____

Weather Conditions

☀️ ☐   ☁️ ☐   🌤️ ☐   🌧️ ☐   🌧️ ☐   🌨️ ☐   🚩 _____   🌡️ _____

Firearm:	
Bullet:	Seating Depth:
Powder:	Grains:
Primer:	
Brass:	
Distance:	

Overall Results

☐ Poor   ☐ Fair   ☐ Good   ☐ Excellent

Notes

_____

_____

_____

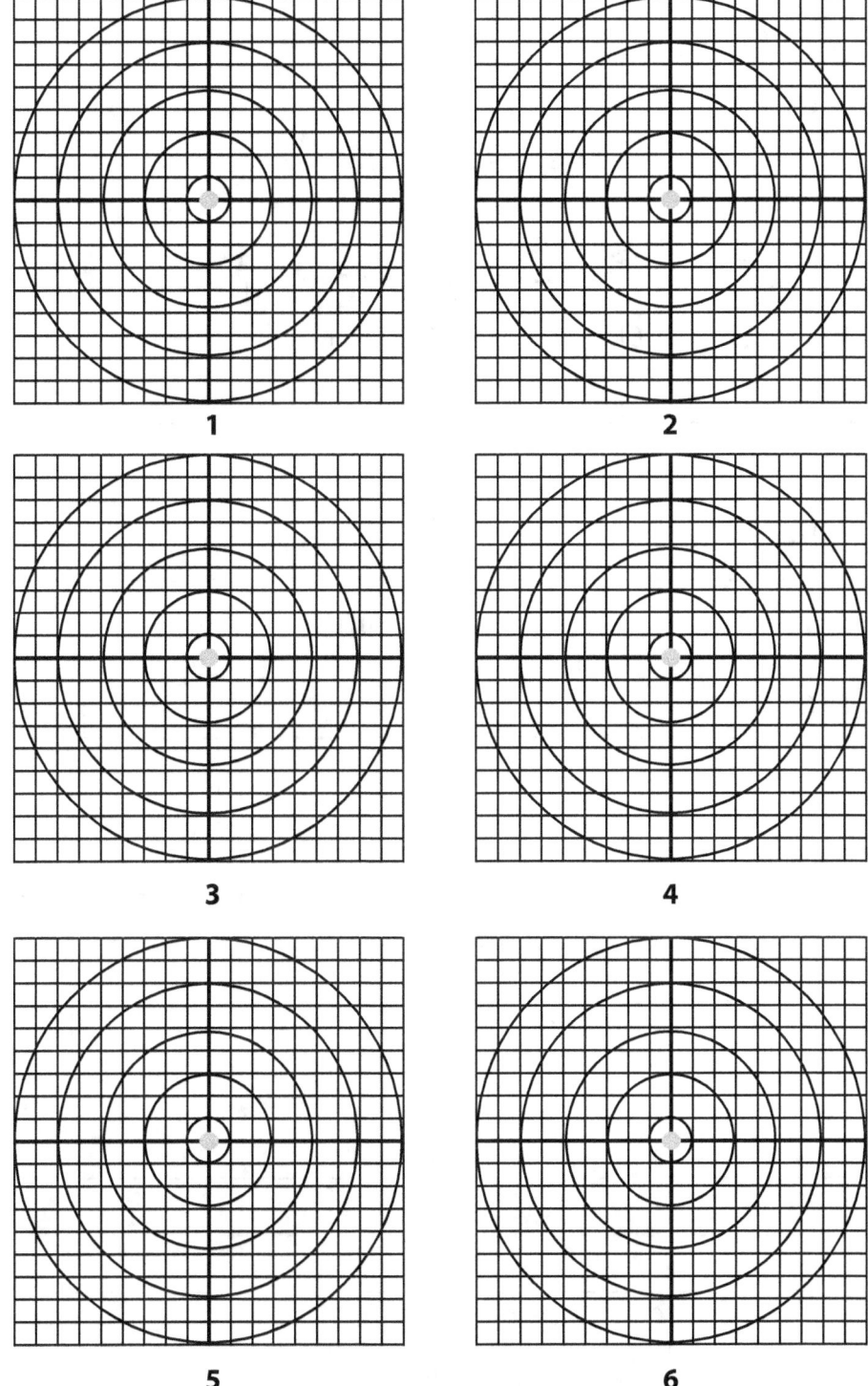

📅 Date: _____ 🕐 Time: _____

📍 Location: _____

Weather Conditions

☀️ ☐ ⛅ ☐ 🌤️ ☐ 🌧️ ☐ 🌧️ ☐ 🌨️ ☐ 🚩 _____ 🌡️ _____

Firearm:	
Bullet:	Seating Depth:
Powder:	Grains:
Primer:	
Brass:	
Distance:	

Overall Results

☐ Poor   ☐ Fair   ☐ Good   ☐ Excellent

Notes

_____

_____

_____

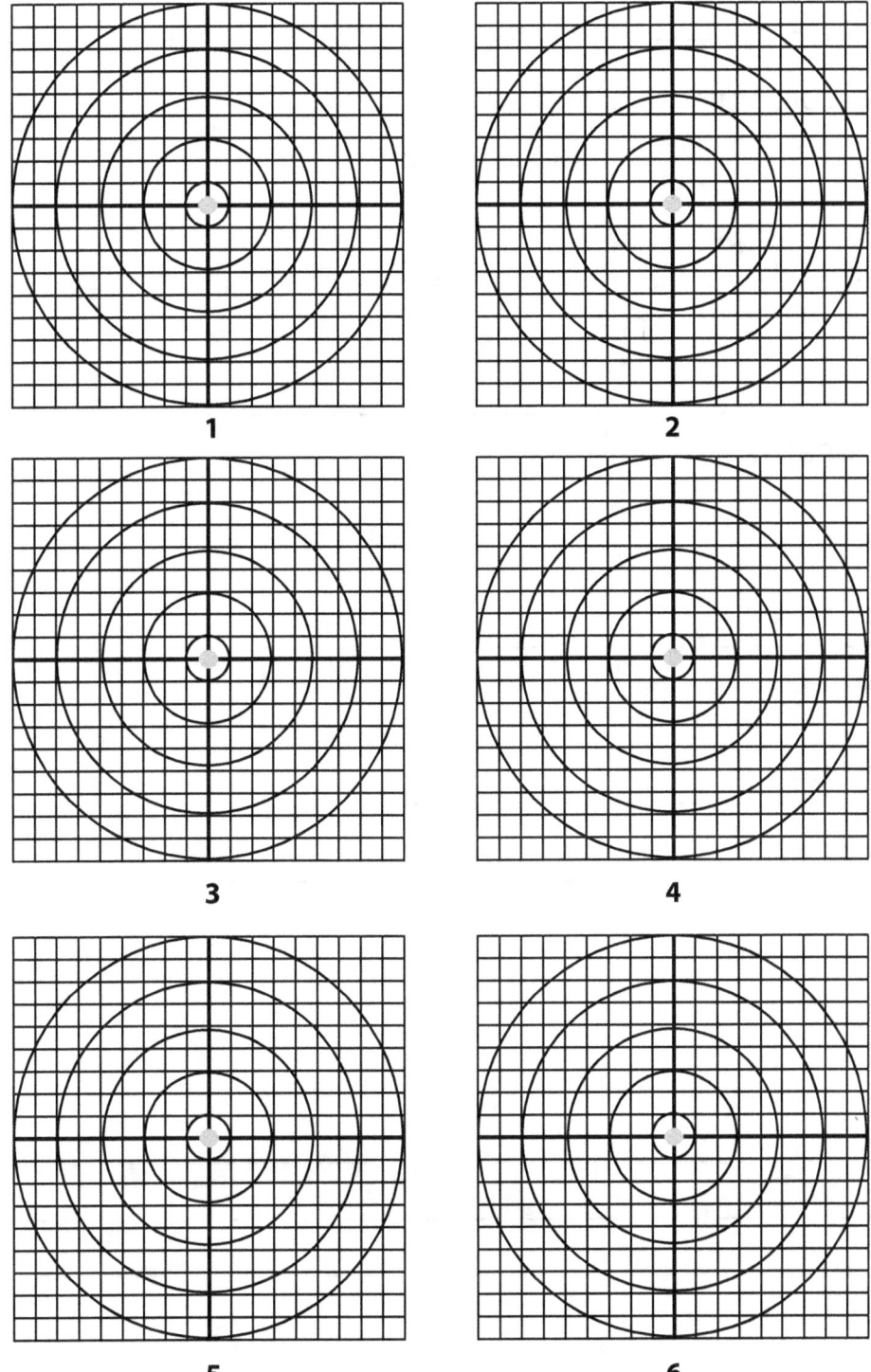

Date: _____   🕐 Time: _____

📍 Location: _____

Weather Conditions

☀ ☁ ⛅ 🌧 🌧 🌨 🚩 🌡
☐   ☐   ☐   ☐   ☐   ☐   ____ ____

Firearm:	
Bullet:	Seating Depth:
Powder:	Grains:
Primer:	
Brass:	
Distance:	

Overall Results

☐ Poor   ☐ Fair   ☐ Good   ☐ Excellent

Notes

_____
_____
_____

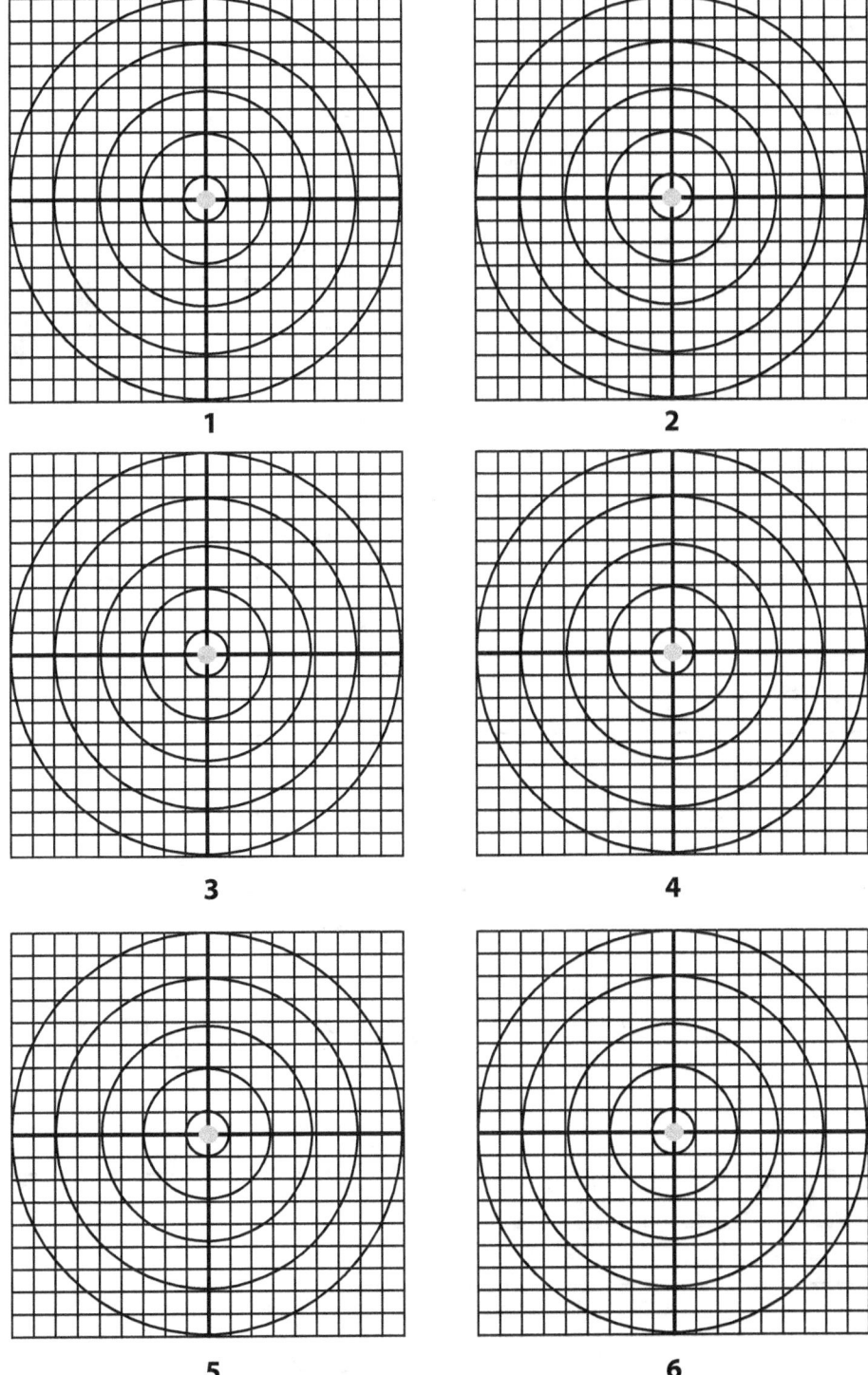

📅 Date: _____ 🕐 Time: _____

📍 Location: _____

Weather Conditions

☀️ ☁️ ⛅ 🌧️ 🌧️ 🌨️ 🚩 🌡️
☐   ☐   ☐   ☐   ☐   ☐   _____   _____

Firearm:	
Bullet:	Seating Depth:
Powder:	Grains:
Primer:	
Brass:	
Distance:	

Overall Results

☐ Poor   ☐ Fair   ☐ Good   ☐ Excellent

Notes

_____

_____

_____

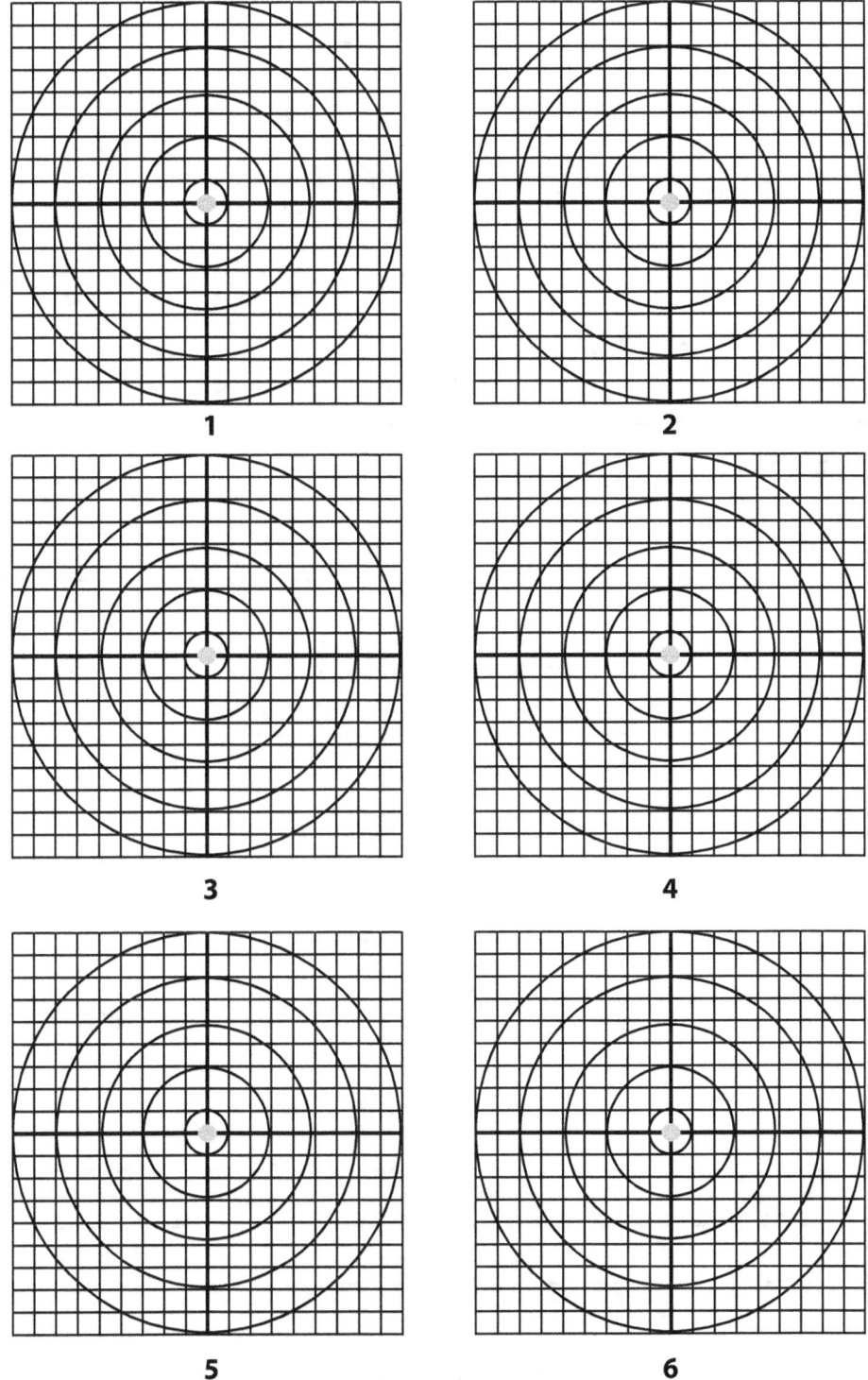

📅 Date: _____ 🕐 Time: _____

📍 Location: _____

Weather Conditions

☀ ☁ 🌤 🌧 🌧 🌨 ⚑ 🌡
☐ ☐ ☐ ☐ ☐ ☐ ____ ____

Firearm:	
Bullet:	Seating Depth:
Powder:	Grains:
Primer:	
Brass:	
Distance:	

Overall Results

☐ Poor   ☐ Fair   ☐ Good   ☐ Excellent

Notes

_____

_____

_____

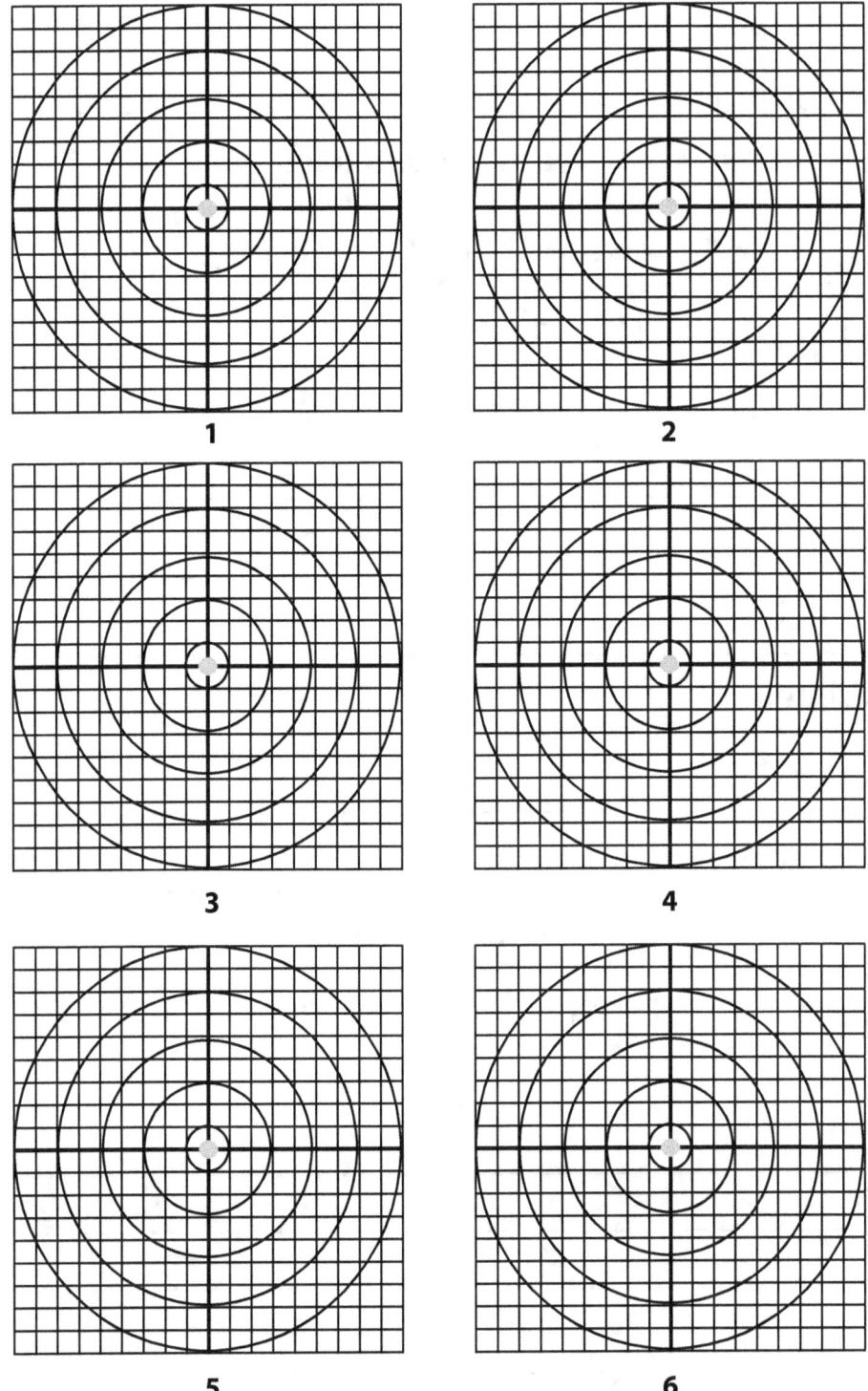

📅 Date: _____ 🕐 Time: _____

📍 Location: _____

Weather Conditions

☀ ☁ ⛅ 🌧 🌦 🌨 ⚑ 🌡
☐ ☐ ☐ ☐ ☐ ☐ _____ _____

Firearm:	
Bullet:	Seating Depth:
Powder:	Grains:
Primer:	
Brass:	
Distance:	

Overall Results

☐ Poor   ☐ Fair   ☐ Good   ☐ Excellent

Notes

_____
_____
_____

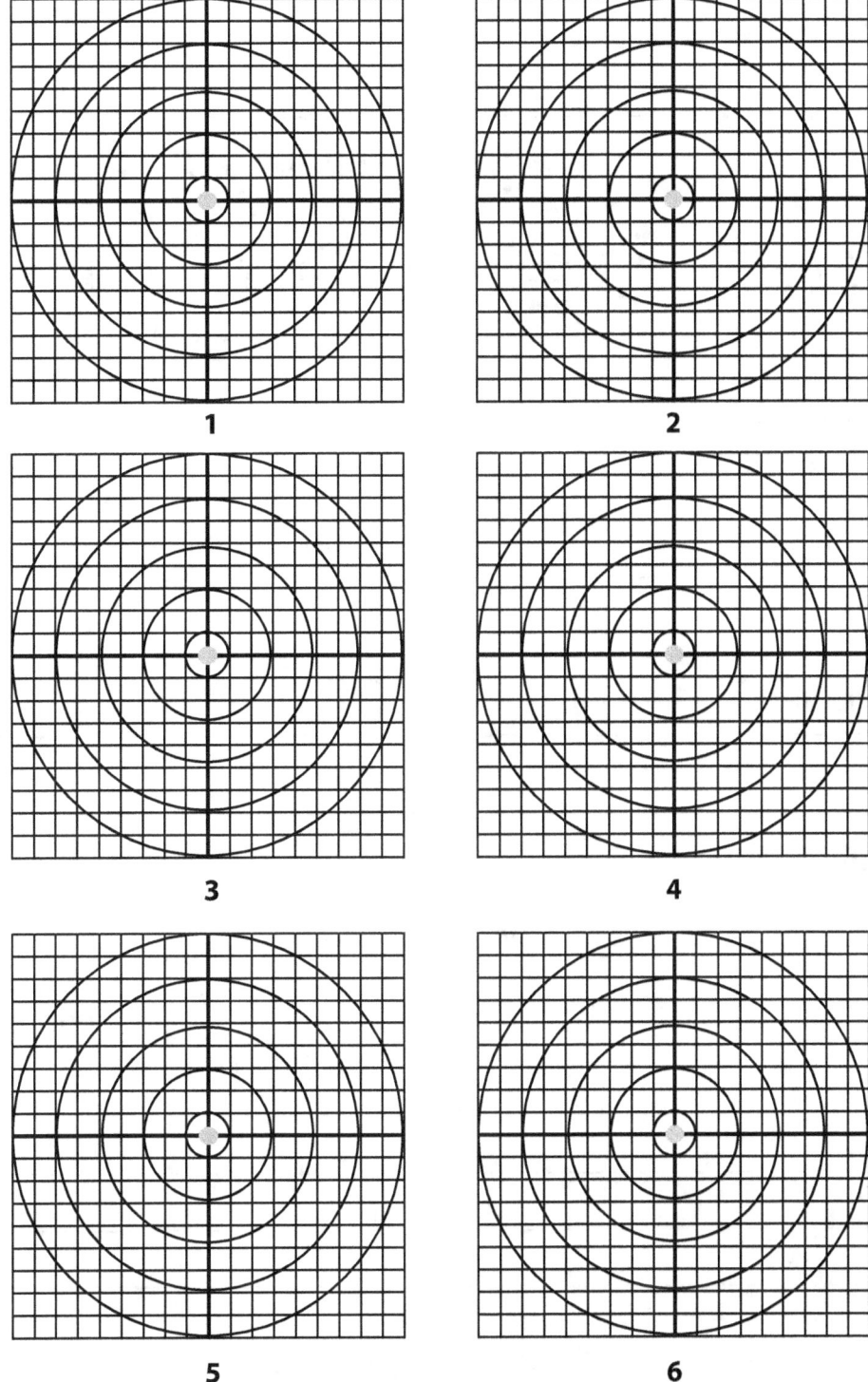

Date: _____ Time: _____

Location: _____

Weather Conditions

☀ ☁ ⛅ 🌧 🌧 🌨 🚩 🌡
☐ ☐ ☐ ☐ ☐ ☐ ____ ____

Firearm:	
Bullet:	Seating Depth:
Powder:	Grains:
Primer:	
Brass:	
Distance:	

Overall Results

☐ Poor   ☐ Fair   ☐ Good   ☐ Excellent

Notes

_____
_____
_____

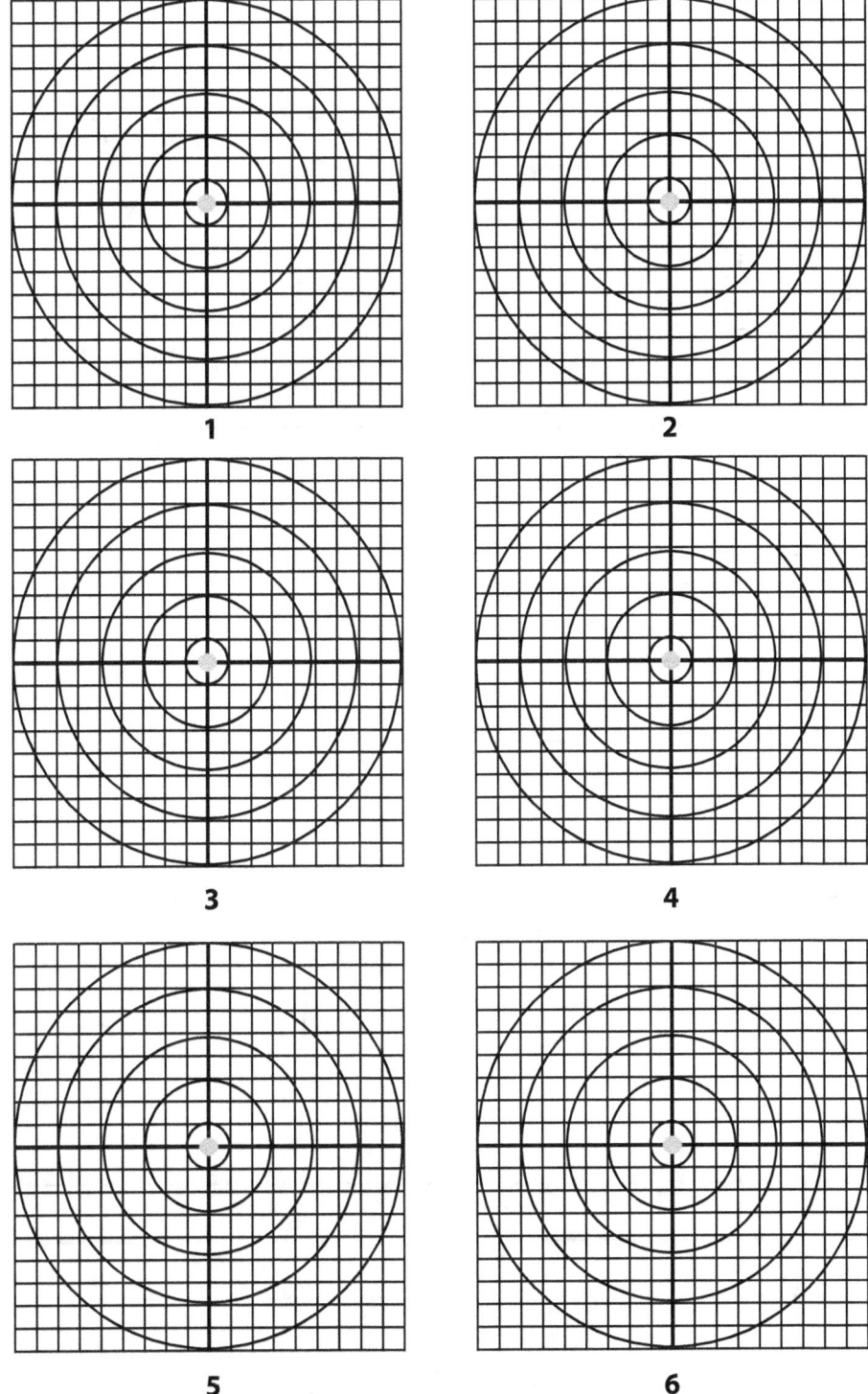

📅 Date: _____   🕐 Time: _____

📍 Location: _____

Weather Conditions

☀️ ☐   ☁️ ☐   🌤️ ☐   🌧️ ☐   🌦️ ☐   🌨️ ☐   🚩 _____   🌡️ _____

Firearm:	
Bullet:	Seating Depth:
Powder:	Grains:
Primer:	
Brass:	
Distance:	

Overall Results

☐ Poor   ☐ Fair   ☐ Good   ☐ Excellent

Notes

_____

_____

_____

☆ ☆ ☆ ☆ ☆

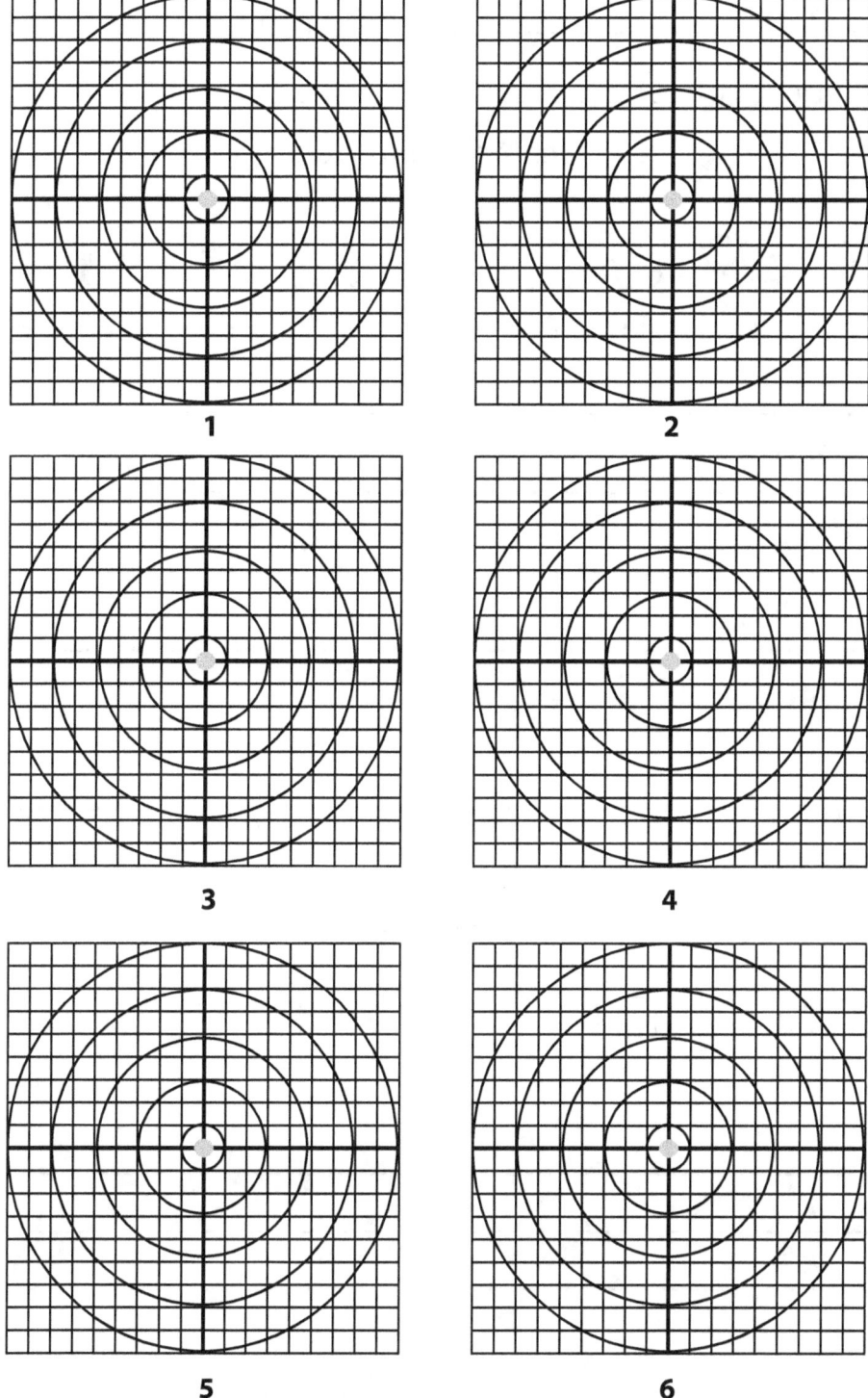

📅 Date: _____   🕐 Time: _____

📍 Location: _____

Weather Conditions

☀ ☁ 🌤 🌥 🌧 🌨 🚩 🌡
☐   ☐   ☐   ☐   ☐   ☐   _____   _____

Firearm:	
Bullet:	Seating Depth:
Powder:	Grains:
Primer:	
Brass:	
Distance:	

Overall Results

☐ Poor   ☐ Fair   ☐ Good   ☐ Excellent

Notes

_____
_____
_____

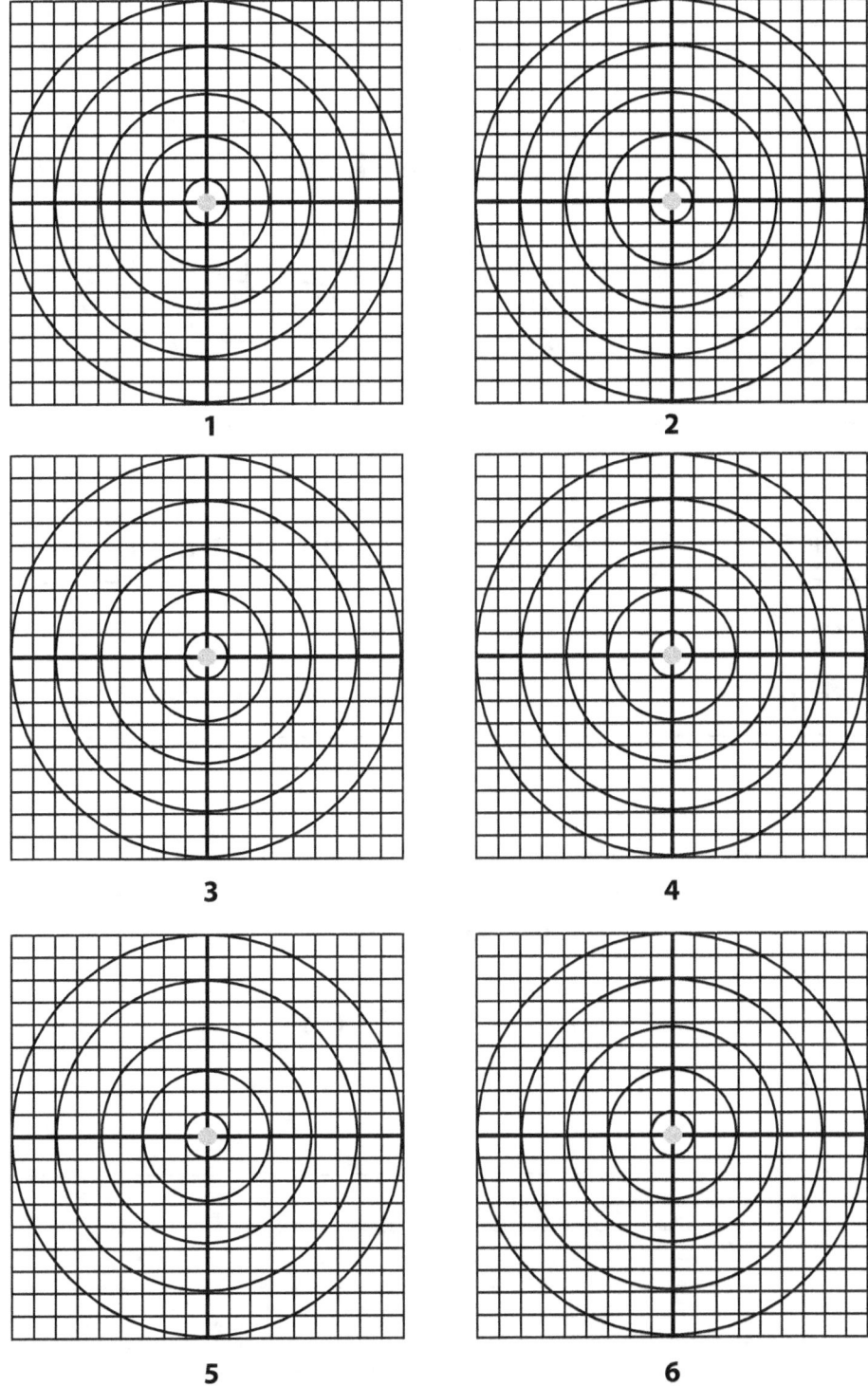

Date: _____ Time: _____

 Location: _____

Weather Conditions

☀ ☁ ⛅ 🌧 🌧 🌨 🚩 _____ 🌡 _____

☐ ☐ ☐ ☐ ☐ ☐

Firearm:	
Bullet:	Seating Depth:
Powder:	Grains:
Primer:	
Brass:	
Distance:	

Overall Results

☐ Poor   ☐ Fair   ☐ Good   ☐ Excellent

Notes

_____

_____

_____

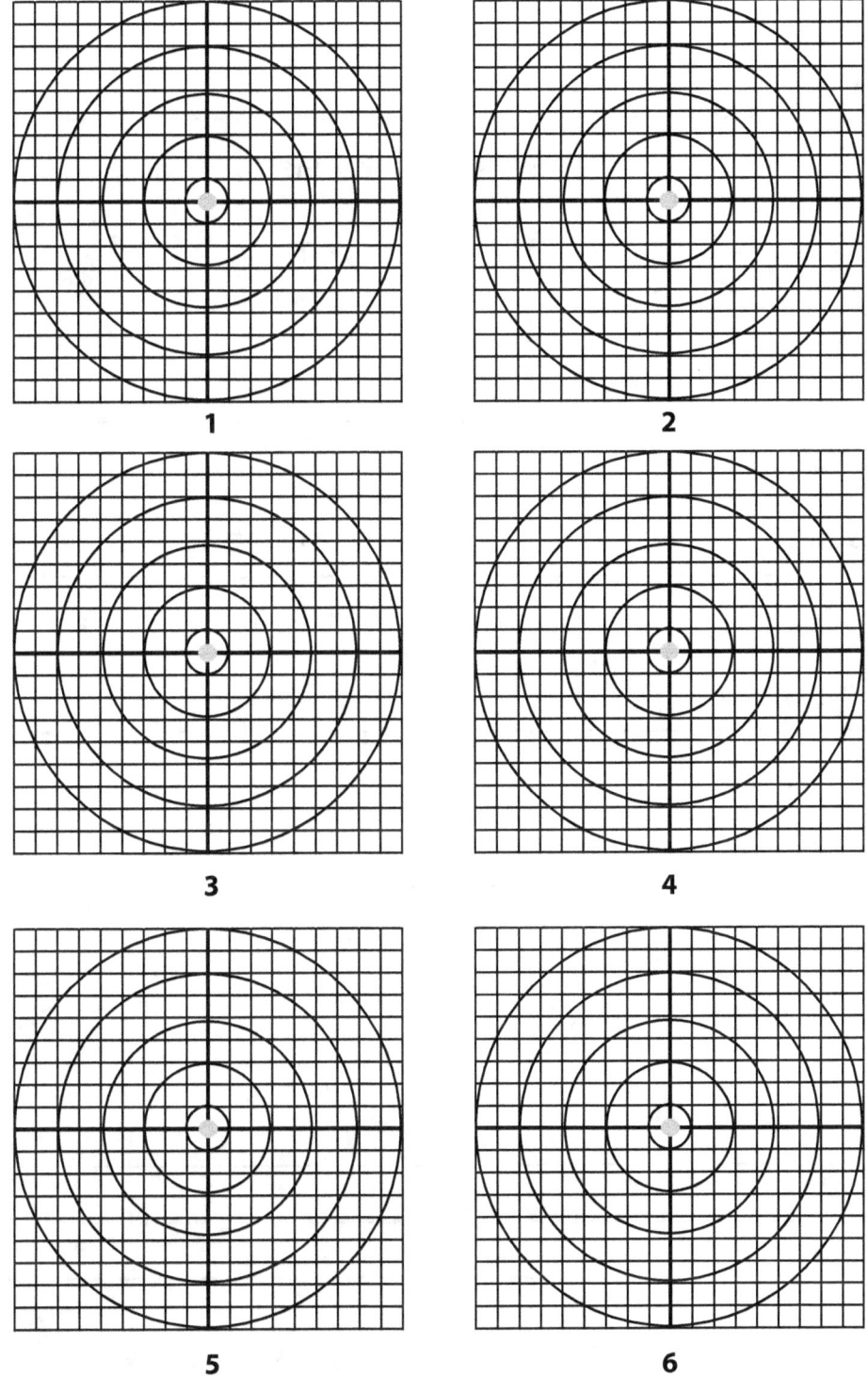

Date: _____ ⏱ Time: _____

📍 Location: _____

Weather Conditions

☀ ☐   ☁ ☐   ⛅ ☐   🌧 ☐   🌧 ☐   🌨 ☐   🚩 _____   🌡 _____

Firearm:	
Bullet:	Seating Depth:
Powder:	Grains:
Primer:	
Brass:	
Distance:	

Overall Results

☐ Poor   ☐ Fair   ☐ Good   ☐ Excellent

Notes

_____

_____

_____

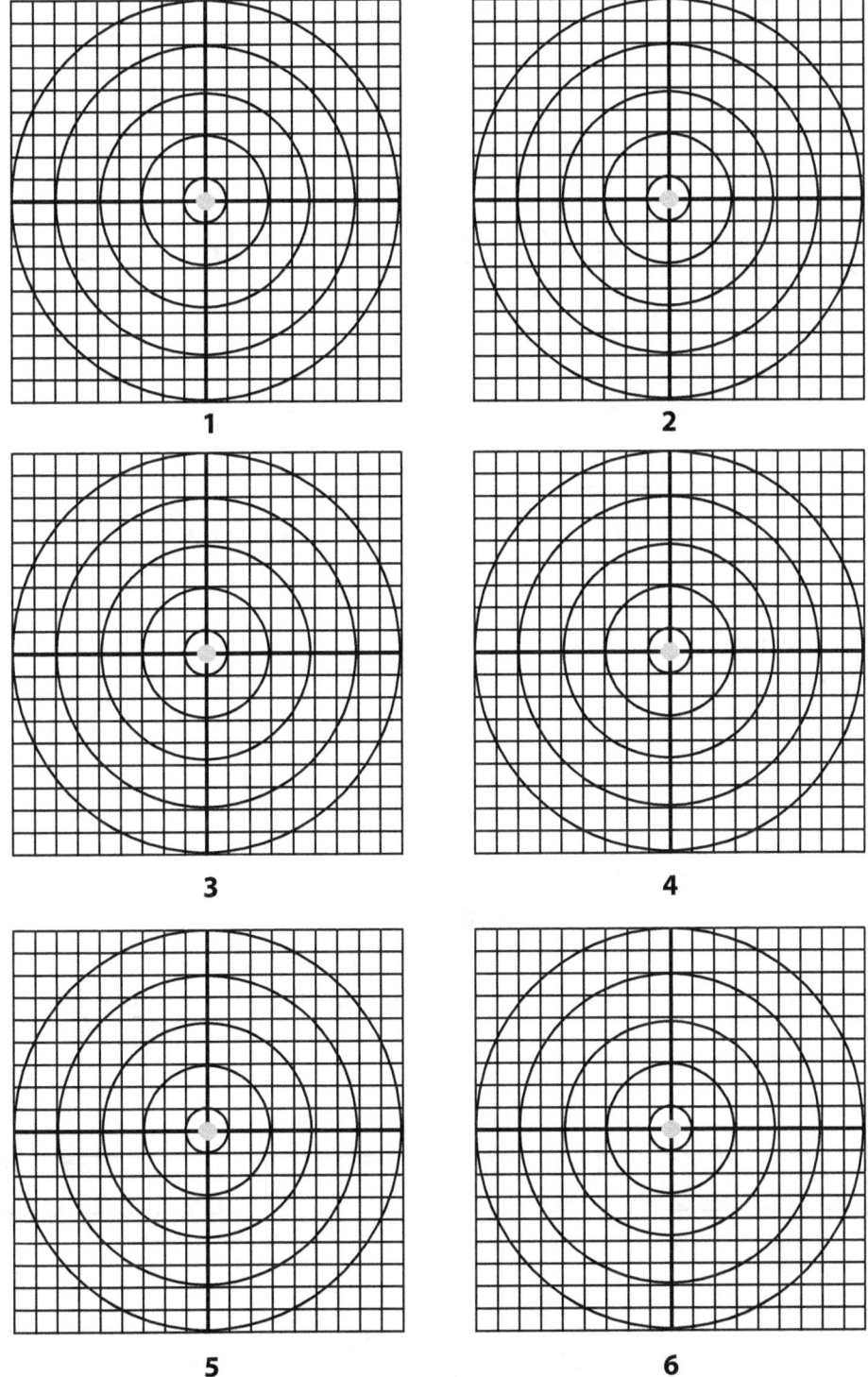

Date: _____ Time: _____

Location: _____

Weather Conditions

☀ ☁ ⛅ 🌧 🌧 ❄ ⚑ 🌡
☐ ☐ ☐ ☐ ☐ ☐ ____ ____

Firearm:	
Bullet:	Seating Depth:
Powder:	Grains:
Primer:	
Brass:	
Distance:	

Overall Results

☐ Poor   ☐ Fair   ☐ Good   ☐ Excellent

Notes

_____

_____

_____

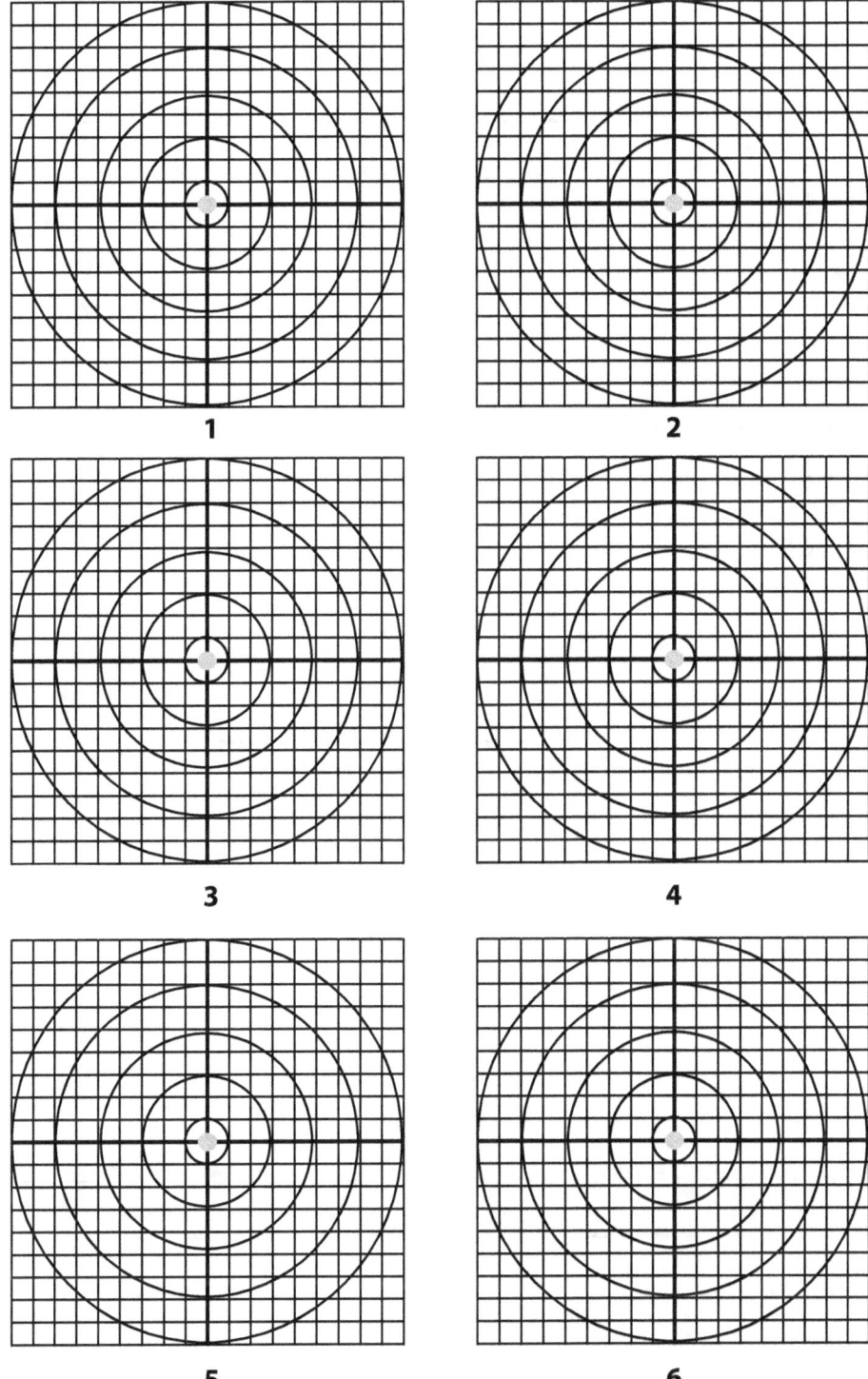

Date: _____ ⏱ Time: _____

📍 Location: _____

Weather Conditions

☀ ☁ ⛅ 🌧 🌧 🌨 🚩 🌡
☐ ☐ ☐ ☐ ☐ ☐ ____ ____

Firearm:	
Bullet:	Seating Depth:
Powder:	Grains:
Primer:	
Brass:	
Distance:	

Overall Results

☐ Poor   ☐ Fair   ☐ Good   ☐ Excellent

Notes

_____

_____

_____

☆ ☆ ☆ ☆ ☆

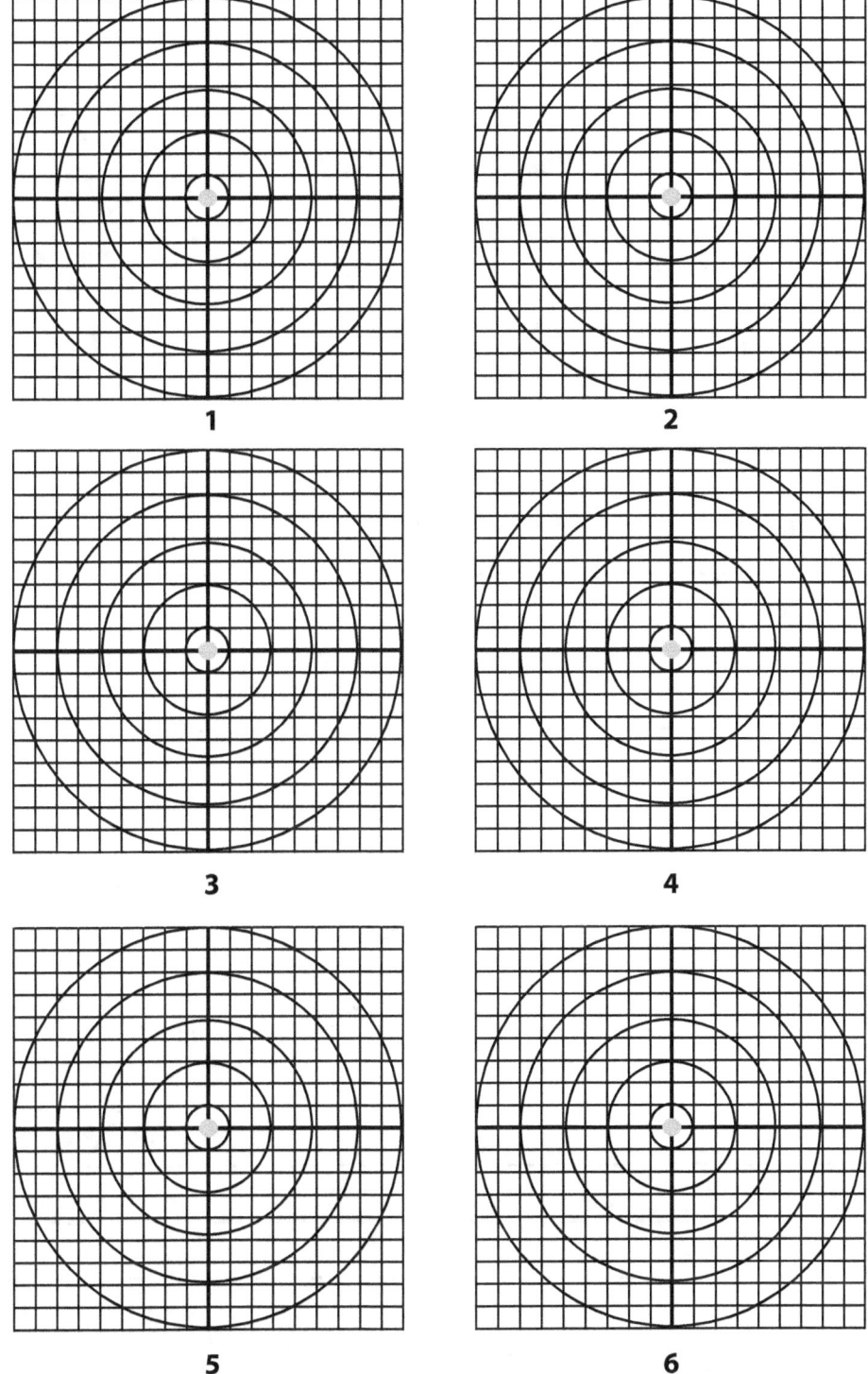

Date: _____ 🕐 Time: _____

📍 Location: _____

Weather Conditions

☀ ☁ 🌤 🌧 🌦 🌨 🚩_____ 🌡_____
☐ ☐ ☐ ☐ ☐ ☐

Firearm:	
Bullet:	Seating Depth:
Powder:	Grains:
Primer:	
Brass:	
Distance:	

Overall Results

☐ Poor ☐ Fair ☐ Good ☐ Excellent

Notes

_____
_____
_____